English Frameworking

The creative literacy course for English at 11–14

Julia Strong
Deputy Director, National Literacy Trust

Pam Bloomfield

Emily Rought-Brooks

National Literacy Trust
Building a literate nation

Published by HarperCollins*Publishers* Limited
77–85 Fulham Palace Road
Hammersmith
London
W6 8JB

www.**Collins**Education.com
On-line support for schools and colleges

ISBN 0 00 711349 8

Julia Strong, Pam Bloomfield and Emily Rought-Brooks assert
their moral rights to be identified as the authors of this work.

British Library Cataloguing in Publication Data
A catalogue record for this publication is available from the
British Library.

Acknowledgements

Text: Extracts from *Design and Technology Food Foundation Course*
and *Collins English Dictionary, Millennium Edition* published by
HarperCollins Publishers. Reprinted by permission of the
publishers, pp7, 9, 41; extract from *Review of Harry Potter and the
Philosopher's Stone*. Reviewed by Lindsay Fraser, for the Scotsman,
28th June 1997. Reprinted with permission of Lindsay Fraser,
Scottish Book Trust, p7; extract from *Brushing Up Our Community*
produced by McDonalds. Reprinted with permission, p7; extract
from *Ten Minute Guide to HTML 4 3E* by Tim Evans. Copyright
1997 by Que Publishing. Reprinted by permission of Que
Publishing, as represented by Penguin Computer Publishing, a
Division of Pearson Education, p7; extract from *Self Assessment
Form* produced by the Inland Revenue. Reprinted with
permission, p7; extract from *Fatu-Hiva* by Thor Heyerdahl,
published by HarperCollins Publishers. Reprinted by permission
of the publishers, p9; extract from *Science Connections 1*
published by HarperCollins Publishers. Reprinted by permission
of the publishers, p9; extract from *Geography 21 - The United
Kingdom* by Simon Ross, published by HarperCollins Publishers.
Reprinted by permission of the publishers, p9; extract from 'The
Sun Says' in *The Sun*, 18th September 2000. Copyright © News
International Newspapers Limited, 18th September 2000.
Reprinted by permission, p9; extract from *Media Skills: An
Introduction* published by Longman, p9; extract from 'The
Flowers' by Alice Walker. Reprinted by permission of David
Higham Associates Limited, p19; extract from *The Ghost Drum*
by Susan Price, published by Faber and Faber Limited. Reprinted
by permission of the publishers, p20; extract from *The Thief of
Always* by Clive Barker, published by HarperCollins Publishers.
Reprinted by permission of the publishers, p21; extract from
Skellig by David Almond, published by Hodder & Stoughton
Limited. Reprinted by permission of the publishers, p23; extract
from 'Dead Language Master' by Joan Aiken, from *Scary! Stories
that will make you scream* edited by P. Haining. Copyright © Joan
Aiken Enterprises Limited. Reprinted by permission of A M
Heath & Co. Limited on behalf of Joan Aiken, p25; extract 'The
Poison Ladies' by H. E. Bates, from *The Watercress Girl and Other
Stories*. Reprinted by permission of Laurence Pollinger Limited
and the Estate of H. E. Bates, p27; extract from *The Papers of The
Revd R. G. Smith*. Reprinted with the kind permission of Mrs. B.
Smith and the Trustees of the Imperial War Museum, p31;
extract from *No Cake, No Jam* by Marian Hughes, published by
Heinemann. Reprinted by permission of Andrew Mann Limited,
p31; extract from *Nelson Mandela* by Benjamin Pogrund,
published by Exley Publications. Reprinted by permission of the
publishers, p31; extract from *Zlata's Diary: A Child's Life in
Sarajevo* by Zlata Filipović published by Penguin UK, translated
by Christina Pribichevich-Zoric (Viking 1994, first published in
France as *Le Journal de Zlata* by Fixot et editions Robert Laffont
1993). Copyright Fixot et editions Robert Laffont 1993, p33;

extract from *Coming to England* by Floella Benjamin, published
by Pavilion Books. Reprinted by permission of Pavilion Books
Limited, p35; extract from *Homer: The Odyssey*, translated by E.
V. Rieu, published by Penguin. Reprinted by permission of
Penelope Rieu, p43; extract from *Dictionary of Classical Mythology*
by Edward Tripp, published by HarperCollins Publishers.
Reprinted by permission of the publishers, p45; extracts from
Dorling Kindersley Encyclopedia of Science, published by Dorling
Kindersley. Reprinted by permission of the publishers, p47;
extract from *Patrick Moore on Mars* published by Cassell & Co.
Reprinted by permission of the publishers, p53; extract from
Special K cereal packet. Reprinted by permission of Kelloggs,
p61; extract from Body Shop leaflet on Skin Defensives.
Reprinted by permission of The Body Shop, p61; extract from a
Center Parcs advertisement. Reprinted with permission of Center
Parcs, p61; extract from *The Sun*, 29th August 2000. Copyright ©
Times Newspapers Limited, 29th August 2000. Used with
permission, p63; Bernard Matthews advert, reprinted with
permission of Bernard Matthews Foods Limited, p67; extract
from *Friends and Enemies* by Anita Naik, published by Hodder &
Stoughton Limited. Reprinted by permission of the publishers,
p69; extract from 'The smack of good sense' by Tom Uttley, in
The Daily Telegraph, 21st May 1999. Copyright © Telegraph
Group Limited, 21st May 1999. Used with permission, p71;
extract from *On Yer Bike!* Produced by London Cycling
Campaign. Reprinted with permission, p71; extract from
Vitamins, Minerals and Supplements produced by Boots The
Chemists. Reprinted with permission, p71; extract from an *IPC
competition* in Woman and Home. Copyright Woman and
Home/IPC Syndication. Reprinted with permission of IPC
Syndication, p71; cartoon *Andy Capp*. Reprinted by permission
of the Mirror, p85; extract from *Twopence to Cross the Mersey* by
Helen Forrester, published by HarperCollins publishers.
Reprinted by permission of the publishers, p88; extract from the
playscript of *Twopence to Cross the Mersey* by Helen Forrester,
adapted as a playscript by Valerie Windsor, p89; extract from
Stand Up, Nigel Barton by Dennis Potter. Copyright © Dennis
Potter 1968. Reprinted by permission of Judy Daish Associates
Limited, pp94-5, 98-9; extract from 'Plucky run not for
everyone' by Eleanor Ringel Gillespie, from *The Atlanta Journal
Constitution*. Reprinted by permission of Copyright Clearance
Center Inc., p105; extract from 'Competitive Dad' written by
Paul Whitehouse, Charlie Higson and Simon Day from *The Fast
Show* BBC2 1994. Reprinted by permission of Alexandra Cann
Representation, p107; extract from *The Pepper-Tree* by Dal
Stivens, p113; extract from 'Great Uncle Crow' by H. E. Bates,
from *Seven by Five*. Reprinted by permission of Laurence
Pollinger Limited on behalf of The Estate of H. E. Bates, p113;
extract from *The Color of Water* by James McBride. Copyright ©
1996 by James McBride. Used by permission of Riverhead Books,
a division of Penguin Putnam, Inc, p115; extract from *English
NC* produced by DFEE. Crown Copyright, p135.

Photos: John Walmsley, pp5, 49, 103, 109, 137; Science Photo
Library, p7 (David Nunuk), p41 (John Sandford), p52 (US
Geological Survey), p55 (NASA); PA photos, pp31, 53; Mary
Evans Picture Library, p44; © Trip/H Rogers, p57;
Bettman/Hulton, p95; BBC, p99; © Bubbles/Jennie Woodcock,
pp125, 137; Hulton Getty, pp145, 148.

Cover and internal design by Ken Vail Graphic Design
Commissioned by Helen Clark
Edited by Rachel Orme-Smith and Kim Richardson
Production by Katie Morris
Printed and bound by Scotprint, UK

Whilst every effort has been made both to contact the
copyright holders and to give exact credit lines, this has not
proved possible in every case.

Internal artwork by Pat Murray, pp10, 47; Steward Lees,
pp12–13; Abigail Conway, p21; Felicity House, pp23, 73, 89,
143; Tony Forbes, pp29, 101; Rhiannon Powell, p36; Paul
McCaffrey, pp81, 83, 111, 129, 139, 141.

NLT website
www.literacytrust.org.uk

Contents and skills matching grid

* key objectives are in bold

Introduction

English Frameworking has been written to help you make the transfer from the literacy hour in primary school to English lessons in secondary school.

You'll find that all the work you've done in the literacy hour will be built on – not just in English but in all the other subjects as well. All the approaches and activities you've been used to will still be there. So your English lessons will begin with clear objectives and include a range of activities – as a class, in groups, as a pair and individually – to help build up your confidence. And at the end of every lesson, you'll review what you've learnt. As this book has been designed to take up from where you left off in primary school, it starts with a short section to help you show your teacher just how much you know.

So what will be different? For a start, there won't be an hour of literacy a day. Instead you'll have around three hours of English a week. Throughout the year, you'll be increasing the range of texts you read as well as developing your powers of discussion and your writing skills in a wide range of styles. You'll be looking at how plays, including television plays and soap operas, are written as well as writing and performing your own scripts and presenting your ideas. And it will help you learn how to perform effectively when you're being tested.

This is the start of five years of learning that will help you become really skilled at reading and writing, speaking and listening. This will open the door for you to have the skills at your fingertips to read and understand about anything that takes your interest, and to enjoy all the wonderful stories and ideas that have been written and told all over the world across the centuries. It will help you to be a good listener as well as a good speaker so that you can join in discussions effectively, considering the views of others, adapting your ideas and arguing your point of view. By the time you get to GCSE age (Year 11), you'll be able to take on many roles and feel confident in any situation that requires you to speak, read or write.

And most of all, you'll have joined in a wide range of entertaining activities which will have helped you enjoy the challenge of learning.

Starting Key Stage 3

Introduction

One of the big challenges of secondary school is for you to be able to understand a vast range of ideas. Many of these will be written down, so being able to get information and enjoyment from text is vital. In addition, you will need to build on your present skills so that you become an expert writer able to understand the purpose and audience of any writing task, and able to structure your own writing in a whole range of styles. Above all, you'll need to be able to discuss your ideas clearly. English lessons will be at the heart of this learning but every subject area will be strengthening your use of language, reading, writing and speaking and listening skills.

Key aim

In this section you will:

- Build on your understanding of the nature of the different types of text, focusing especially on non-fiction text, and some of the key vocabulary that relates to this.

Different types of text

Aims

On these two pages you will:
- Build on your understanding of the nature of the different types of non-fiction text.
- Consider the vocabulary that relates to this.

Starter *as a class*

How many different texts have you come in contact with so far today – from the moment you saw the cereal packet or the toothpaste tube? You've got one minute to jot down your ideas before you brainstorm ideas as a class.

Introduction *as a class*

Remember the literacy hour you did in primary school? Now you're going to find out how much you've remembered about the language you used. Listen carefully when the words in the grid on **Worksheet 1** are read to you. They will be read first on their own, and then in a sentence to give you the context.

- If you've never heard the word before, tick the first column.
- If you've heard the word before but can't remember what it means, tick the second column.
- If you think you know what it means, jot down your explanation in the third column.

When you've finished, add up the number of entries in your columns. Not all of these words will be covered today, but by the end of this section, you should be confidently using all of them.

Development *as a class*

1 Listen and watch carefully while your teacher presents six different texts to you (**Worksheets 2–3**). As a class, you should answer the following questions about each text:
- What is its purpose?
- Who is the audience?
- What type of text is it?
- What is its structure and layout?
- What is its style (language features)?

Watch carefully as your teacher **annotates** one of the texts to highlight the key points, because you're going to be doing this yourselves in an activity on pages 14–15.

> **annotate** mark up with your own notes

as a group

2 Each group will be allocated one of the extracts on page 7. Discuss the extract in preparation for presenting your ideas about it to the class using the following five categories:
- Purpose
- Audience
- Text type
- Structure and layout
- Style (language features).

Representatives from each group should present the group's findings to the class as if they are the teacher, so don't forget to use the appropriate language. To start the presentation, a member of your group should read the extract to the class.

Plenary

Review the key questions that you need to ask when you analyse text.

1

"*Harry Potter and the Philosopher's Stone* has all the makings of a classic … Rowling uses classic narrative devices with flair and originality and delivers a complex and demanding plot in the form of a hugely entertaining thriller. She is a first-rate writer for children."
The Scotsman

2

Aristotle, 384–322 BC, Greek philosopher; pupil of Plato, tutor of Alexander the Great, and founder of the Peripatetic school at Athens; author of works on logic, ethics, politics, poetics, rhetoric, biology, zoology and metaphysics. His works influenced Muslim philosophy and science and medieval scholastic philosophy.

4

The most dramatic recollections I had were the sights themselves. Of all the spectacular views we had, the most impressive to me was on the way to the Moon, when we flew through its shadow. We were still thousands of miles away, but close enough so that the Moon almost filled our circular window. It was eclipsing the Sun, from our position, and the corona of the Sun was visible around the limb of the Moon as a gigantic lens-shaped or saucer-shaped light, stretching out to several lunar diameters. It was magnificent, but the Moon was even more so.

3

Shouldering the responsibility

Ask what concerns people about our world and their answer is often – the environment. Ask what annoys them about their own area and they often reply – litter.

We all share a responsibility to look after our world and to care for our local community – but how many of us actually do anything about it?

Everyone can play a part – and together, we can make a world of difference.

5

Q14: *Do you want to claim relief for pension contributions?*

Do not include contributions deducted from your pay by your employer to their pension scheme, because tax relief is given automatically. But do include your contributions to personal pension schemes and free-standing AVC schemes.

6

Download Disappointment

Users sometimes wait for several minutes while a video or audio file downloads, and then nothing happens, or an error message occurs. This is usually an indication that the multimedia format isn't supported on your computer, the Web browser wasn't set up to use the correct Helper application/plug-in, or the Helper application plug-in was not installed. Some recent browsers will ask you what to do with the data, while in some cases you'll be prompted to download the necessary plug-in on the spot.

Analysing texts

Aims

On these two pages you will:

- Understand the main features of the key types of text.
- Strengthen your understanding and use of the key vocabulary relating to non-fiction.
- Make clearly organized notes that you can use later to support speaking.
- Understand how the meaning of words is built up from separate parts.

Starter *as a group*

All words have a main part or *stem*: this is the most important bit of the word to look at when you want to work out its meaning. Often other bits of meaning are added on to this stem either in front of it (*prefix*) or after it (*suffix*), as in the example below:

prefix	*stem*	*suffix*	*suffix*
unhelpfully un	help	ful	ly

1   Each group will be given two envelopes containing several cards (**Worksheet 4**). Envelope A contains cards with the stem 'tract', and cards with prefixes or suffixes. Envelope B contains shaded cards. Put all the cards saying 'tract' one above the other so that they form a column. Now add prefixes and suffixes to 'tract' and see how many words you can make.

2   Now see if you can match the prefixes to the meanings on the shaded cards from envelope B. Think of other words that begin with the same prefix to help you work out the meaning.

3   Be prepared to feed back your ideas to the rest of the class.

4   How could breaking down words like this help you with your spelling and understanding of words?

Introduction *as a class*

Listen carefully while your teacher demonstrates how to analyse text 1 below.

Development *as a group*

In your group, look at the six different types of text on page 9. Sort the texts into the categories named on the grid on **Worksheet 5**. Once you think you've categorized the text, then fill in the grid to sum up your findings, jotting down notes on the purpose, audience, structure and style.

Plenary

Each group should feed back their ideas on the different texts to the rest of the class. Don't be afraid to question other people's ideas. See if each group agrees on the key ingredients of each of the texts. Remember to use the appropriate vocabulary wherever possible.

1

Several times the boat was almost filled with gushing water and it was as if we were sinking into the sea. But soon it rose once more, the bundles of bananas floating in sea water, while all the rowers bailed for their lives. The excitement was hectic, without a moment of repose.[1] Time and again I abandoned all hope as we raced along the wall of a breaking swell …

[1] *rest*

2

SOLID

ENERGY

LIQUID

ENERGY

GAS

Particles in a solid are fixed in regular patterns and cannot move much – they just wobble, or *vibrate*. When you add energy to a solid, the particles vibrate faster. When they are vibrating quickly enough, they can break away from their fixed positions. They are still close together but can slide over each other. The solid melts into a liquid.

3

Write down all the tasks that need to be done, then put them in order. Draw a box around each task. You may be able to group related tasks together in one box. The boxes show the stages in the making process. Link these together with arrows. Fig. 1.52 shows a block diagram for making an apple crumble. Use the method listed in your recipe to work out all the stages you will need to complete.

4

Northumberland National Park is one of the most remote and wild of the National Parks. The park stretches from Hadrian's Wall in the south to the border with Scotland in the north. It is a working National Park with farming being the main activity. Most of the park is privately owned, but quite a large part is owned by the Ministry of Defence and used for military training.

The National Park is popular with both locals and tourists because there are many things to see and do.

5

THE SUN SAYS

Yesterday's opinion polls, one of which put the Tories ahead of Labour, are quite simply devastating.

They prove beyond a shadow of a doubt that The Sun was right all last week and the Prime Minister was WRONG.

They prove this Government is now in dangerous waters.

They prove it is now entirely possible that Tony Blair is going to be ditched by the British people at the next election.

6

This is not an ordinary baby!

When Nasreddin's wife died, he married again. His new wife was a widow.

A week after he married her, she had a baby.

Nasreddin at once went to the market and bought some paper, some pencils and some children's books. He came back home with these things and put them beside the baby.

His wife was surprised. "What are you doing?" she said. "The baby won't be able to use those things for a long time. Why are you in such a hurry?"

"You are quite wrong," answered her husband. "Our baby is not an ordinary baby. It came in a week instead of nine months. You see, it will be ready to learn to read and write in a few weeks from now."

7

Throughout this century, it has been argued that the media have had a strong direct effect on audiences. Earlier in the century it was believed wartime propaganda and later Nazi propaganda in Germany were examples of this influence. In the 1950s, advertising was seen as persuading people to buy products in ways they did not realise.

Instructions and descriptions

Aims

On these two pages you will:

- Experiment with different types of writing (instructions and descriptions) that present similar material and compare the results.
- Give clear instructions when writing.
- Make clearly organized notes that you can use later to support your writing.

Starter

Watch carefully as your teacher makes toast and keep in mind the order in which all the actions take place.

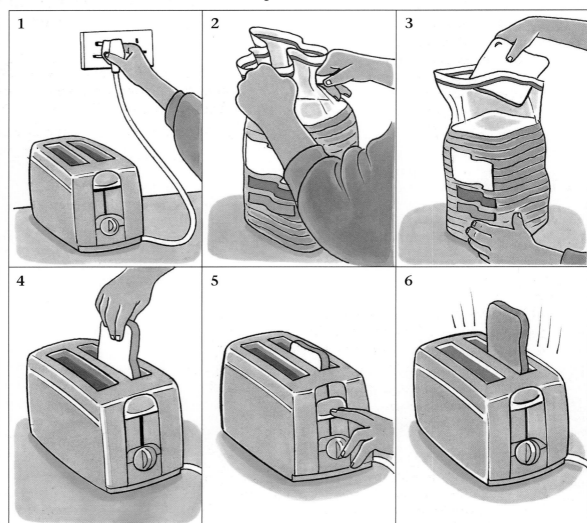

Introduction

1 Write down a clear set of instructions for making toast. Check yours against your neighbour's and see if you need to make any **amendments**.

> **amendment**
> alteration, change, improvement

 as a class

2 Listen carefully while some of the instructions that you have written are read out. Discuss which are best and why. As a class, make a list of the ingredients for good instruction writing.

Development

1 Your teacher is going to make some more toast. Think carefully about what you can see, hear, smell, feel and taste when bread is being toasted. Now fill in the grid on **Worksheet 6** while you experience the sights, sounds, smells, touch and taste of toast being made.

2 Select your best words and phrases and share them with the class. Discuss what makes them effective descriptive words.

3 Use the words and phrases you've selected from this grid in a piece of creative writing, describing someone making a piece of toast. Use your whiteboards or a piece of paper to help **draft** really powerful sentences.

as a class

4 Listen carefully while your teacher reads out a selection of the written work and discuss what makes the writing effective.

> **draft** to produce an early version of a piece of written work

Plenary

Be prepared to explain the key differences between writing instructions and descriptive writing, and note down the key features of each.

homework

Think of anything that you know how to make (for example, food, or an object like a model car) or anything you know how to use (for example, a microwave or a mobile phone).

- Write a short paragraph describing this object as vividly as you can.
- Then write brief instructions about how to make or use it.

> ! **Remember** to read your work carefully, improve it if necessary, and write a brief comment on how well you think you have completed the task.

Strategies for recount writing

Aims

On these two pages you will:

- Investigate how a range of strategies is used in an effective recount text.
- Think about key sentences and summing up information.

Starter  on your own

In this lesson you will be reading an extract from a book called *Longitude* by Dava Sobel. You may find the extract a bit of a challenge, as it's quite difficult at times. But it's worth the effort because it is wonderful writing which deals with all sorts of things – extraordinary behaviour, bravery, a hanging, many deaths, murder and guilt – and, best of all, it's true.

To help you out, some of the tricky words from the story have been listed below. Do you know what all of them mean? You will be assigned one of these words; use a dictionary to find out its meaning.

Write the word and its definition on a piece of A4 paper which can be displayed on your classroom wall.

skirmishes

consensus

depletion

peninsula

demise

contrition

misgauged

quintessential

longitude

saga

location

hulls

subversive

scurvy

mutiny

purportedly

Introduction *as a group*

Working in groups of three, you will be given an envelope containing the extract from chapter 2 of *Longitude* (**Worksheet 7**).

1 Each person in the group should take two paragraphs from the six in the envelope. Work out if the text in your two paragraphs is in chronological order and whether one of them may be the opening or the closing paragraph of the whole extract. If you think you have the opening or closing paragraph, read it to your group and see if you all agree. What evidence is there to support your view?

2 Now, in your group, **sequence** the text and decide what sort of text it is. Feed back your ideas to the rest of the class and establish the correct order for the passage and how you know you're right.

> **sequence** to put into a logical order

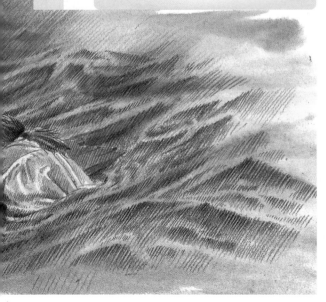

Development *as a group*

1 Identify where the writer moves away from chronological order and decide why she has done so.

2 List any other features that make the passage interesting.

3 Most of the events in the paragraph beginning 'Only two men' happened before the ship smashed into the rocks. How does the reader know this?

4 What **connectives** has the writer used in the paragraph beginning 'Only two men …'? Are they effective?

5 The paragraph beginning 'Only two men' contains the word 'his' seven times and the word 'he' four times. Work out who 'he' and 'his' refers to in each case and how the writer has made this clear.

6 This passage describes what happened all too often to sailors in an age when they were not able to plot their position accurately on a sea chart. Which sentence sums up the consequences of this situation?

7 Sum up what this passage tells you about life on board a ship in 1707.

Be prepared to report back on these questions.

> **connective** a word or phrase that links clauses or sentences and signals in which direction the ideas in the sentences are moving. Examples are 'also', 'however', 'besides', 'therefore' and 'later'.

Plenary

Feed back your findings to the class, and review the typical features of recount writing.

Presenting text

Aims

On these two pages you will:

- Revise all that you've learnt about the six key types of writing that you've focused on and the language that goes with them.
- Consider the types of text you've come across in other subject areas.
- Become the teacher and present a text to the rest of the class, using evidence and illustration to support your ideas. You've got half the lesson to get yourself prepared.
- Make clearly organized notes that you can use later to support your speaking.
- Learn about your school's spelling log.

Starter *as a class*

1 Listen carefully while your teacher reads out some of the homeworks that you did describing an object that you could make or use (page 11). Discuss what makes these good examples.

 2 Your teacher will explain to you how your school's spelling log works. Look at the spellings that have been corrected in your work, and at the spelling strategies in your spelling log, and see if you can come up with suggestions for how to remember these words.

3 Now spend a few minutes looking through your own work and at your teacher's comments on it and decide on three more ways in which you could improve it.

Introduction *as a group*

In this section you have focused on some of the key vocabulary that relates to non-fiction text. See how many of these words you can remember. Watch carefully as your teacher shows you how to play word dominoes (**Worksheets 8a, 8b**). You have to be able to explain the technical link between the words to join one domino to another. Be prepared to explain your links to your teacher or to the group next to you.

chronological

prefix

suffix

structure

paragraph

colloquial

Development as a group

Now you're going to go back to the seven passages you started categorizing on pages 8–9. But this time each group is going to focus on one passage in detail. You've got about ten minutes to prepare for the challenge of commenting on the purpose, audience, text type, structure and style of your text at the OHP as if you were the teacher. Just to remind you how to do this, the example you saw in the first lesson (pages 6–7) will be on the OHP to help you.

An important part of your preparation will be annotating the OHT of your text (**Worksheet 9**). Remember that you can only use the notes on your OHT to help you for the final presentation. You might find the sentence starters below useful:

	Suggested openers
Purpose and audience	● We think the purpose of this text is ... ● The audience for this text would be ...
Text type	● We think that text x is ... text because ... ● We couldn't decide whether text x is ... or ... because ... ● You can tell this is recount writing because ... ● This could be an autobiography or someone writing as if ...
Structure/form	● The information is presented in chronological order which suggests that ... ● This is structured like a short story because ... ● The way each paragraph is introduced tells you that ...
Style (language features)	● This is written in the 1st/2nd/3rd person, which has the effect of ... ● This passage is full of description which ... ● The writer repeats phrases like ... because ...

Remember, though, that each text will be different – many of these suggestions will not suit your text. Each person in the group should take one heading from this speaking frame to focus on and practise what they are going to say.

Plenary

Think of all the different types of text you have encountered in your first few weeks at secondary school. What types of text have you been reading and writing in each of your subject areas?

Reviewing what's been learnt

In this section you have increased your understanding of the nature of the different text types, focusing on non-fiction texts, and all the key vocabulary that relates to them. In particular:

- You have looked in more detail at recount text.
- You have considered the difference between instructions and descriptive writing.
- You have made notes on an OHT and used them to present your ideas on a text to the class, and you may have had to defend your viewpoint not just in a small group but in front of the whole class.
- You have listened while others have presented their ideas and you may have questioned their conclusions.

Reflect on what you've learnt from this section and then, in your exercise book, write targets to improve your work. You should consider the following areas:

- Spelling
- Vocabulary
- Sentence structure
- Planning your writing
- Reading
- Speaking and listening.

My targets to improve my work are:

-
-
-
-
-
-

Imagine, explore, entertain

Introduction

When you imagine, you form a picture in your mind of something, whether it is of a place, a person or a feeling. You can use your imagination to help you understand what it would be like to be someone else, or to live in another country or time, or you can use it to create a fantasy world where anything can happen.

Reading and writing stories or 'fiction' is a good way of using your imagination. In fiction anything is possible so you can let your imagination run away with you. Literary non-fiction – text based on real events in people's lives – includes personal records and other accounts of events that have happened. Reading other people's diaries, journals, letters and autobiographies allows you to imagine and explore what it would be like to be someone else, or to live in another place or time.

In this section you will explore the main features and ingredients of good fiction and literary non-fiction writing and use them in your own writing.

Key aim

In this section, you will:

- Understand more about how to read and write effectively in a wide range of narrative and recount styles.

Plot

Aims

In these two pages you will:

- Explore the concept of genre, and revise some common literary genres.
- Think about what makes a good story.
- Develop your understanding of how a story is structured.
- Read a short story, thinking about the **plot** and exploring its meaning.

plot the storyline of a novel or play

Starter
as a class

Your teacher will explain how your school's reading record works. You will use this to record all the different types of things (genres) you read, and what you like reading best. You probably used the word 'genre' in primary school to refer to different categories of text such as narrative, recount or explanation.

Genre is also often used to refer to a kind or style of art or literature. In drama, for example, you may get tragedy, comedy or satire. There are different genres of novels such as horror, romance and science fiction. Genre can also refer to categories of writing such as poetry, novels and drama.

Your teacher will give you some cards and an activity to test your ability to identify different genres (**Worksheet 10**).

Introduction
as a class

Have you ever read a book that is so good that you can't put it down? What was it about and what made it so entertaining? As a class, discuss what you think makes a good story, using the following bullet points as a starting point:

- Plot
- Character
- Setting
- Style.

A strong and interesting plot is an important ingredient of a good story. Stories generally follow a similar format:

Introduction

This needs to grab the reader's attention and make them want to read on by giving clues about what might happen in the story. It sets the mood and atmosphere of the story.

Developing plot

The plot will then move on to develop the ideas set out in the introduction. More details will be revealed about characters, settings and action. This part of the plot needs to hold the reader's attention by giving hints of the crisis to follow.

Complication

Plots usually have a complication or 'problem' which adds interest and uncertainty to the plot.

Crisis

The crisis is the climax of the story, which the plot has been building up to.

Resolution

This is the end of the story, when the crisis has been overcome and the problems have been sorted out. All the loose ends in the plot are tied up.

Development *as a group*

The extract on the right is the first part of a short story by Alice Walker called 'The Flowers'. Listen to the extract being read to you, then discuss the following questions in groups of four:

1 *Introduction* (paragraphs 1–2)
- What do you learn about Myop here?
- How do you know that this story is set in another country?
- What atmosphere has the author created here? Pick out words from the paragraph to support your view.
- Is there anything in the second paragraph to suggest that something important is about to happen to Myop?

2 *Developing plot* (paragraphs 3–5)
- What descriptions confirm that this story is set in another country? Where do you think it is set?
- How do the last two lines in the last paragraph add to a sense that something is about to happen to Myop? What do you think it might be?

3 *Crisis and resolution* (paragraphs 6–8)
- Now listen to the rest of the story and discuss the questions on **Worksheet 11**.

Plenary

Discuss your answers as a class. Can you come up with a sentence summing up what the message of the story is?

Why do you think Alice Walker constructed this story the way she did?

Add this story to your reading record.

It seemed to Myop as she skipped lightly from hen house to pigpen to smokehouse that the days had never been as beautiful as these. The air held a keenness that made her nose twitch. The harvesting of the corn and cotton, peanuts and squash,[1] made each day a golden surprise that caused excited little tremors to run up her jaws.

Myop carried a short, knobby stick. She struck out at random at chickens she liked, and worked out the beat of a song on the fence around the pigpen. She felt light and good in the warm sun. She was ten, and nothing existed for her but her song, the stick clutched in her dark brown hand, and the tat-de-ta-ta-ta of accompaniment.

Turning her back on the rusty boards of her family's sharecropper[2] cabin, Myop walked along the fence till it ran into the stream made by the spring. Around the spring, where the family got drinking water, silver ferns and wild-flowers grew. Along the shallow banks pigs rooted. Myop watched the tiny white bubbles disrupt the thin black scale of soil and the water that silently rose and slid away down the stream.

She had explored the woods behind the house many times. Often, in late autumn, her mother took her to gather nuts among the fallen leaves. Today she made her own path, bouncing this way and that way, vaguely keeping an eye out for snakes. She found, in addition to various common but pretty ferns and leaves, an armful of strange blue flowers with velvety ridges and a sweetsuds bush full of the brown, fragrant buds.

By twelve o'clock, her arms laden with sprigs of her findings, she was a mile or more from home. She had often been as far before, but the strangeness of the land made it not as pleasant as her usual haunts. It seemed gloomy in the little cove in which she found herself. The air was damp, the silence close and deep.

[1] *a vegetable*
[2] *a tenant farmer who gives part of each crop as rent*

Alice Walker is a highly acclaimed African-American author. She was born in 1944 in Georgia in the United States. During the 1960s she was actively involved in fighting for the rights of black people in America. Her most well-known book, *The Color Purple*, was published in 1982. It won the Pulitzer Prize for Fiction and has since been made into a film.

Aims

In these two pages you will:
- Explore the narrative devices used by authors to make their writing enjoyable.
- Focus on imagery, especially personification, as a way of creating vivid pictures in writing.
- Use these narrative devices in a short piece of writing of your own.

Starter  on your own

Today you're going to look at some of the tricks writers use to help the reader picture the scene being described. At primary school you will have done work on **imagery** and probably used the terms **metaphor** and **simile**. Below are two similes and two metaphors. Can you work out which is which and explain the difference?

- Snow blanketed the icy ground.
- Snow covered the ground like a blanket.
- Rain bucketed down on our heads.
- It was raining as if a bucket of water was being poured over our heads.

Many writers prefer metaphor to simile because it is more direct. You're going to use **Worksheet 12** to focus on a type of metaphor called personification.

> **imagery** the use of language to create a vivid image or picture
> **metaphor** a form of imagery when one thing is said to be another
> **simile** a form of imagery when one thing is compared with another

Introduction as a class

The way a story is written is just as important as the plot. Authors have a number of tricks, or 'devices', that they use to make their writing as enjoyable as possible. The extract below is taken from a mythical story by Susan Price called *The Ghost Drum*. Listen carefully while this extract is read to you.

The author uses several narrative devices to keep the reader interested. They are listed on **Worksheet 13**, along with some questions about them for you to discuss.

In a place far different from where you are now grows an oak-tree by a lake.
  Round the oak's trunk is a chain of golden links.
5 Tethered to the chain is a learned cat, and this most learned of all cats walks round and round the tree continually.
  As it walks one way, it sings songs.
  As it walks the other, it tells stories.
10 This is one of the stories the cat tells.
My story is set (says the cat) in a far-away Czardom, where the winter is a cold half-year of darkness.
  In that country the snow falls deep and lies
15 long, lies and freezes until bears can walk on its thick crust of ice. The ice glitters on the snow like white stars in a white sky! In the north of that country all the winter is one long night, and all that long night long the sky-stars
20 glisten in their darkness, and the snow-stars glitter in their whiteness, and between the two there hangs a shivering curtain of cold twilight.

From *The Ghost Drum* by Susan Price

Susan Price had her first book published when she was sixteen. As well as writing she has worked as a guide in a museum.

Now read the second extract below. Try to find examples of the narrative devices the author has used and what effect these devices create. Use the grid on **Worksheet 14** to record your responses.

The great grey beast February had eaten Harvey Swick alive. Here he was, buried in the belly of that smothering month, wondering if he would ever find his way out through the cold
5 coils that lay between here and Easter.
He didn't think much of his chances. More than likely he'd become so bored as the hours crawled by that one day he'd simply forget to breathe. Then maybe people would wonder why
10 such a fine young lad had perished in his prime. It would become a celebrated mystery, which wouldn't be solved until some great detective decided to recreate a day in Harvey's life.

From *The Thief of Always* by Clive Barker

Clive Barker has written 18 books, many of which are horror and fantasy stories. He also produces and directs films for television and cinema.

Development on your own

Look at the way Clive Barker describes the month of February in the second extract. Think of the weather that you like the least. Make a list of things that you dislike about it and think of as many **adjectives** as you can to describe this weather. If the weather was an animal what animal would it be?

Write a short passage describing your weather as if it were that animal. You may find the sentences that you created in the starter activity useful. Remember to use some or all of the following narrative devices:

- Imagery
- Repetition
- Descriptive language
- Varied sentence length.

adjective a word that describes something: 'the <u>tall</u> cupboard', 'the <u>round</u> balloon'

! *Remember* to read your work carefully, improve it if necessary, and write a brief comment on how well you think you have completed the task.

Plenary

Look over your descriptive passage. Your teacher will ask some of you what narrative devices you have used and why, so be prepared to identify them and explain why you used them.

Use the skills you have developed to write a descriptive passage entitled 'The Worst Weather I Can Remember'.

Setting

Aims

In these two pages you will:

- Explore how writers use descriptive language to create an effective setting for their stories.
- Use these descriptive devices in a piece of writing of your own.
- Use expanded noun phrases to enhance your descriptions.

Starter *as a class*

Sometimes when we're describing things we just use one adjective with a noun, such as the black dress, or the new sports centre. When you use adjectives and nouns together you make what is known as a **noun phrase**.

You may, however, want to add a bit more information to this noun phrase to expand your description. Have a look at the sentences below:

- *The old cat watched the bird.*
- *The old cat under the tree watched the bird.*
- *The old cat hiding under the tree watched the bird.*
- *The old cat, who was hiding under the tree, watched the bird.*

You will notice that the adjective 'old' comes in front of the noun 'cat', but all the other phrases that expand the noun phrase come *after* the noun.

Expand the noun 'man' in the following sentence in the same way.

- *The man waited for the train.*

You'll notice that David Almond uses a whole variety of these expanded noun phrases in the extract from *Skellig* that you're about to read.

Introduction *as a class*

Another important ingredient of a good story is the setting. A successful setting depends upon good descriptions which build up a clear and vivid picture in the reader's mind. To help them do this, writers often appeal to some or all of the five senses:

- Sight
- Hearing
- Touch
- Smell
- Taste.

You used these five senses when you were describing toast on pages 10–11 in the opening section. By bringing the reader's senses to life the setting seems real. This helps the reader to experience what the characters experience.

in pairs

Discuss with a partner what you may be able to see, hear, touch, smell and taste if you were standing in a queue waiting for your school dinner. If you were going to describe this scene to someone else what would you tell them?

on your own

Now you're going to see how David Almond in his story *Skellig* helps the reader to picture a crumbling garage. The narrator, Michael, and his family have just moved into their new house which has an old crumbling garage at the bottom of the garden. Michael's parents feel that it may collapse and have forbidden him to enter it. But Michael ignores their instruction.

noun phrase a group of words in a sentence that functions in the same way as a noun

Read the extract opposite. Then use the copy of it on **Worksheet 15** to highlight any description that you think is particularly effective. Write brief notes to the side of it explaining why it works. See if the parts you find effective refer to any of the five senses. Be prepared to present your ideas to the class.

Development *on your own*

First listen and watch carefully while your teacher models for you how to describe a scene effectively. Be prepared to offer suggestions for how sentences could be made more powerful.

Now it's your turn. Write a one-paragraph description of a place you remember well.

● Describe what it looked like, and what smells, sounds, feelings and tastes you remember.

● Use descriptive language, including adjectives, precise nouns and descriptive verbs.

● If possible use imagery to create a picture in the reader's mind.

> **!** **Remember** to read your work through carefully, correcting any errors and redrafting sentences that could be improved.

Plenary

Identify two aspects of your paragraph that are good examples of the descriptive devices you have been exploring. Be prepared to share what you have written in a class discussion.

> *Skellig* was David Almond's first novel, for which he won the Whitbread Children's Book of the Year and the Carnegie Medal.

There were old chests of drawers and broken wash-basins and bags of cement, ancient doors leaning against the walls, deck chairs with the cloth seats rotted away. Great rolls of rope and cable hung from nails. Heaps of water pipes and great boxes of rusty nails were scattered on the floor. Everything was covered in dust and spiders' webs. There was mortar that had fallen from the walls. There was a little window in one of the walls but it was filthy and there were rolls of cracked lino standing in front of it. The place stank of rot and dust. Even the bricks were crumbling like they couldn't bear the weight any more. It was like the whole thing was sick of itself and would collapse in a heap and have to get bulldozed away.

Something little and black scuttled across the floor. The door creaked and cracked for a moment before it was still. Dust poured through the torch beam. Something scratched and scratched in a corner. I tiptoed further in and felt spiders' webs breaking on my brow. Everything was packed in tight – ancient furniture, kitchen units, rolled-up carpets, pipes and crates and planks. I kept ducking down under the hose-pipes and ropes and kitbags that hung from the roof. More cobwebs snapped on my clothes and skin. The floor was broken and crumbly. I opened a cupboard an inch, shone the torch in and saw a million woodlice scattering away. I peered down into a great stone jar and saw the bones of some little animal that had died in there. Dead bluebottles were everywhere. There were ancient newspapers and magazines. I shone the torch on to one and saw that it came from nearly fifty years ago. I moved so carefully. I was scared every moment that the whole thing was going to collapse. There was dust clogging my throat and nose. I knew they'd be yelling for me soon and I knew I'd better get out. I leaned across a heap of tea chests and shone the torch into the space behind and that's when I saw him.

Aims

In these two pages you will:

- Explore how writers portray characters through description and action.
- Write your own short description of a character.
- Practise using subordinate clauses to make your writing more interesting.

Starter  as a class

Read the following extract and discuss what's wrong with this sort of writing:

> I got up and got dressed and then I realized it was a bit late. I had a quick breakfast and left for school. I reached school just as the bell rang. I went straight to my tutor room and then sat down.

Watch carefully while your teacher models for you how to use **subordinate clauses** to make this sort of writing more interesting, using the following sentences (**Worksheet 16**).

> - Jo was late for school.
> - She forgot to set the alarm.

Very soon it's going to be your turn. In a few minutes you may be modelling for the class how to join the following sentences:

> - The teacher looked up crossly.
> - John walked in late.

Introduction in pairs

Another important ingredient of a good story is the characters. The characters need to be realistic and believable, otherwise they won't hold our interest.

When writing about or studying the main character in a story, there are some key points that you need to think about:

- What the character looks like
- What the character says and thinks
- How the character behaves
- What other characters say or think about them.

Thinking about these various points will help you to build up a complete picture of what a character is like.

In this lesson you will look at the ways in which characters are portrayed through description. In the next lesson (pages 26–27) you will look at what you can learn about characters through the dialogue.

The extract on page 25 is taken from a short horror story called 'Dead Language Master' by Joan Aiken. What do you learn about Mr Fletcher from this description? Working in pairs, read the extract and use the grid on **Worksheet 17** to record your responses.

Why do you think the writer chose the title 'Dead Language Master'?

> **subordinate clause** a clause that adds information to, or qualifies, the main clause of a sentence

Mr Fletcher taught us Latin. He was the shape of a domino. No, that's wrong, because he wasn't square; he looked as if he had been cut out of a domino. He had shape but no depth, you felt he could have slipped through the crack at the hinge of a door if he'd gone sideways. Though I daresay if he'd really been able to do that he would have made more use of the <u>faculty</u>;[1] he was great on stealing quietly along a passage and then opening the door very fast to see what we were all up to; he used to drift about silently like an old ghost, but if you had a keen sense of smell you always had advance warning of his arrival because of the capsule of stale cigarette smoke that he moved about in. He smoked nonstop; he used a holder, but even so his fingers were yellow up to the knuckles and so were his teeth when he bared them in a horse-grin. He had dusty black hair that hung in a <u>lank</u>[2] flop over his big square forehead, and his feet were enormous; they curved as he put them down like a duck's flippers, which, I suppose, was why he could move so quietly … If someone kicked up a disturbance at the back of the classroom he'd first screw up his eyes and stick his head out, so that he looked like a snake, weaving his head about to try and focus on the guy who was making the row; then he'd start slowly down the aisle, thrusting his face between each line of desks; I can tell you it was quite an unnerving performance …

None of our lot cared greatly for Latin, we didn't see the point of it, so we didn't have much in common with old Fletcher. We thought he was a funny old coot, a total square – he used words like 'topping' and 'ripping' which he must have picked out of the *Boy's Own Paper* in the nineteen-tens. He was dead keen on his subject and would have taught it quite well if anyone had been interested; the only time you saw a wintry smile light up his yellow face was when he was pointing out the beauties of some <u>construction</u>[3] in <u>Livy</u>[4] or <u>Horace</u>.[5]

[1] *ability*	[3] *sentence construction*
[2] *long and limp*	[4, 5] *Latin authors*

Joan Aiken was born in 1924, reportedly in a haunted house. The British author has produced many works of fiction in different genres: plays, poems, novels and short stories, many of which focus on the strange and terrifying.

Development *on your own*

Now it's your turn to write a short description of a character. It can be based on someone you know, such as a teacher you remember from primary school, or the annoying person who always sits next to you on the bus. Before writing your description, brainstorm your ideas using a mental mapping diagram like the one below.

Your teacher will show you how to use your whiteboards or a piece of paper to draft a character portrayal.

> ! **Remember** to read your work through carefully, correcting any errors and redrafting sentences that could be improved. Make certain you've linked your sentences in an interesting way. Get rid of any excess use of 'and' and 'then'. Finish with a brief comment summing up how well you think you have completed the task.

Plenary

Swap your character portrait with a partner's. Go through the checklist (below) to see how many ways your partner has used to bring his or her character to life. Can you suggest any ways of improving the description?

- Are we told what the character looks like?
- Are we told what the character says or thinks?
- Are we told how the character behaves?
- Are we told what other people say or think about the character?

Dialogue

Aims

In these two pages you will:

- Explore how dialogue can be used to bring characters to life.
- Read a short story, concentrating on the effect of the dialogue.
- Practise using a dictionary with speed.

Starter  on your own

Listen carefully while your teacher reads you a short extract from Anne Fine's book *How to Write Really Badly* (**Worksheet 18**). It has a useful hint about finding words in the dictionary quickly. You're going to see if it works in this starter activity.

In the short story you're going to read later in this lesson, the writer has deliberately repeated the words 'Ben said' to stress the childishness of the narrator at the time of the incident and his belief in Ben.

Use Anne Fine's trick to look up 'said' in your dictionary. See if you can be the first one in the class to find it.

There are hundreds of alternative words for 'said'. See if you can be the first to find the alternatives your teacher will now give you.

Introduction on your own

The final element to consider before you write your own short story is how to make your characters come alive through **dialogue**.

Four tips for writing effective dialogue:

1. Put in enough **direct speech** to let the reader picture the characters but not so much as to be boring.
2. For variety, direct speech can be mixed with **indirect speech**.
3. Good writers use dialogue to reveal more about a character. They don't tell us directly what they think about a character, but they let the character reveal it indirectly through his or her words.
4. In order for dialogue to be realistic and believable, it needs to reflect the way people actually speak. This often involves using **informal language** in which the rules of **Standard English** are relaxed. Realistic dialogue may also reflect the **dialects** in which many people speak.

dialect a variety of English, often based on region, which has distinctive grammar and vocabulary

dialogue a conversation between two people, which may be spoken or written

direct speech a way of writing down speech which uses the actual words spoken, e.g. '"I'm tired," said Dave.'

indirect speech (also known as reported speech) a way of writing down speech where the words are referred to indirectly, e.g. 'Dave said he was tired.'

informal language language that includes colloquial language, slang and the use of contracted forms of words, e.g. 'Don't you eat no poison berries.'

Standard English the type of spoken and written English that should be used when formal English is appropriate, e.g. all the explanations and instructions on this page.

Follow carefully while your teacher reads you the first section of 'The Poison Ladies' by H. E. Bates (below). While you are listening to the story, think about the answers to these questions:

1 What features help to make this dialogue realistic and believable?

2 How do you know that the narrator hero-worshipped Ben? (Which lines would you quote as evidence for this?) Why is this more powerful than being told that the narrator worshipped Ben when he was a boy?

3 Why does Ben say 'Akky Duck'? Is this effective?

4 What do you think is going to happen?

Development as a group

Follow carefully while your teacher reads you the end of the story (**Worksheets 19a, 19b**), and use the grid on **Worksheet 20** to help you to analyse the text. Add this story to your reading record.

Plenary

Has H. E. Bates followed the 'Four tips for writing effective dialogue' (page 26) in 'The Poison Ladies'? Find one example of each tip, and share these in a class discussion.

When you are only four, seven is a hundred and five inches are a mile.

Ben was seven and I was four and there were five inches between us. Ben also had big brown leather patches on the seat of his moley corduroy trousers and dark hairs on his legs and a horn-handled knife with two blades, a corkscrew and a thing he called a stabber.

'Arter we git through the fence,' Ben said, 'we skive round the sloe bushes and under them ash trees and then we're in the lane and arter that there's millions and millions o' poison berries. Don't you eat no poison berries, will you? Else you'll die. I swallered a lot o' poison berries once and I was dead all one night arterwards.'

'Real dead?'

'Real dead,' Ben said. 'All one night.'

'What does it feel like to be dead?'

'Fust you git terrible belly ache,' Ben said, 'and then your head keeps going jimmity-jimmity-jimmity-bonk-bonk-bonk-clang-bang-jimmity-bonk-clang-bonk all the time.'

'I don't want to be dead,' I said, 'I don't want to be dead.'

'Then don't eat no poison berries.'

My blood felt cold.

'Why don't we start?' I said. I knew we had a long way to go; Ben said so.

Ben got his knife out and opened the stabber.

'I got to see if there's any spies fust,' Ben said. 'You stop here.'

'How long?'

'Till I git back,' Ben said, 'Don't you move and don't you shout and don't you show yourself and don't you eat no poison berries.'

'No,' I said. 'No.'

Ben flashed the knife so that the stabber pierced the blackberry shade.

'You know Ossy Turner?' he said.

'Yes,' I said. 'Yes.'

Ossy had a hare-lip and walked with one drawling foot and a crooked hand. I always felt awfully sorry for Ossy but Ben said:

'Ossy's like that because he come down here and dint look for spies fust – so they got him and done that to him.'

'Who did?'

Ben was crawling away on hairy knees, flashing the stabber in the sunlight, leaving me alone.

'The Poison Ladies,' Ben said, 'what live down here. In that house I told you about. The two old wimmin what we're going to see if we can see.'

It was fifty years before Ben came back. I knew quite well it was fifty years; I counted every one of them.

'No footmarks,' Ben said.

'I didn't eat any poison berries. I didn't–'

'Let's have a look at your tongue!'

My tongue shot out like a frightened lizard. With big white eyes Ben glared down my throat and said:

'All right. We're going now. Hold your breath.'

'How far is it now?'

'Miles,' Ben said. 'Down the lane and past the shippen and over the brook and then up the lane and across the Akky Duck.'

I didn't know what the Akky Duck was; I thought it must be a bird.

'It's like bridges,' Ben said. 'It's dark underneath. It's where the water goes over.'

'Do the poison ladies live there?'

'They come jist arterwards,' Ben said. 'We hide under the Akky Duck and arter that you can see 'em squintin' through the winders.'

The veins about my heart tied themselves in knots as I followed Ben out of the blackberry shade, over the fence, into the lane and past black bushes of sloe[1] powderily bloomed with blue fruit in the sun.

---

[1] *a small blue-black fruit*

H. E. Bates (1905–1974) was an English writer of short stories and novels, including *The Darling Buds of May*, *The Triple Echo* and *The Snow Goose*.

Writing a story

Aims

On these two pages you will:

- Plan and write a story of your own, thinking about all the ingredients of story writing that you have explored in this section.
- Practise using a thesaurus with speed.

Starter *as a class*

Today you're going to be using all your writing skills to create your own short story. But before you start you're going to use a thesaurus to help you select the right word for your story.

Remind yourself of what an entry in a thesaurus looks like by looking at the example below. Discuss all the features of this entry with a partner, and make sure you know what they are for.

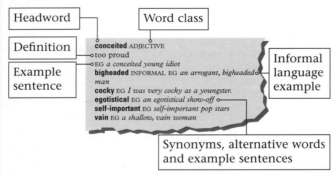

Headword

Word class

Definition

Example sentence

conceited ADJECTIVE
too proud
EG *a conceited young idiot*
bigheaded INFORMAL EG *an arrogant, bigheaded man*
cocky EG *I was very cocky as a youngster.*
egotistical EG *an egotistical show-off*
self-important EG *self-important pop stars*
vain EG *a shallow, vain woman*

Informal language example

Synonyms, alternative words and example sentences

Many thesauruses also have an index. If the word you're looking for is not included in the headwords, you may find it in the index, which will point you to alternative words in the headword section of the thesaurus. For example, you may want to find an alternative for the word 'wrath'. If it isn't listed as a headword in the main part of the thesaurus, you can look it up in the index, where 'rage' and 'anger' are given as alternatives. This also tells you that you will find the word 'wrath' under the headwords 'rage' and 'anger', which will provide more information about it.

on your own

1 Think of three common words that you might want to use when writing a short story (for example, 'said', 'went', 'then') and write them down on your whiteboard or a piece of paper.

2 Use your thesaurus to look these words up and find alternative words. See if you can be the first to find the alternatives. Remember to use the index if you can't find the word among the headwords.

Introduction *in pairs*

Now it's your turn to write your own story. First of all, think about something that happened to you when you were younger – something that seemed very important at the time. Or make something up. Then recount the event to your partner – you will find that as you are talking you remember more and more details.

When you have heard your partner's story, you will probably want to ask some questions, either to clarify details ('I don't understand what you meant when …') or to ask for more details ('So what did your mum say when you got home?') Answering these questions will help you get further into the story.

Development (on your own)

You are now going to plan and write your story using the main story ingredients you have covered in this section. Use the planning frame on **Worksheet 21** to help you to plan your story, and use your whiteboard or a piece of paper to help you draft powerful sentences (see **Worksheet 13** and pages 20–21).

You should:

- Use some of the tricks of the trade (narrative devices) to make your writing vivid.
- Make certain you've linked your sentences in an interesting way.
- Think about the characters and how to bring them alive.
- Make their dialogue reflect their personality and sound realistic.
- Use a thesaurus to ensure that your vocabulary is wide and varied.

> **!** *Remember*, when writing dialogue:
>
> - All direct speech should open and close with speech marks:
>   'Real dead?'
> - If direct speech is followed by a **reporting clause**, add a comma before the closing speech mark:
>   'Real dead,' Ben said.
> - If the sentence continues after the reporting clause, add a comma before the opening speech mark:
>   'Fust you git a terrible belly ache,' Ben said, 'and then your head …'

reporting clause the clause that shows who speaks the words in direct speech, and sometimes how they speak them

Plenary (in pairs)

Swap your story so far with your partner's and see if they have any advice to give about how you could improve your story.

homework

Complete your story for homework.

> **!** *Remember*, when you have finished, read your work through carefully, correcting any errors and redrafting sentences that could be improved. Finish with a brief comment summing up how well you think you have completed the task.
> When your story has been marked, don't forget to add any spelling corrections to your spelling log and think which strategies will help you get them right next time.

Types of literary non-fiction

Aims

In these two pages you will:

- Identify and discuss the features of literary non-fiction texts.
- Work out some spelling rules so that you can add common suffixes to words correctly.

Starter as a group

As you already know, **suffixes** can be added on at the end of words to alter the meaning of the word. In general, adding suffixes is straightforward because you simply add the suffix onto the existing word. In many cases, however, you need to adapt the spelling of the base word when you add the suffix.

In groups of four, look at the words on **Worksheet 22** and see if you can work out a spelling rule for each group of words. Be prepared to feed your ideas back to the class.

 Look at your spelling log. See if any of the words that have caused you problems will be helped by the rules you've just been working on.

suffix a group of letters that can be added to the end of a word to change its meaning or function, e.g. -able, -est, -ly

Introduction as a class

Have you ever wondered what it would be like to live in another country or to be someone else, like a famous footballer? Literary non-fiction – text based on real events in people's lives – gives you a chance to imagine what it would be like to live in another place, time or situation by giving you a glimpse into the lives, thoughts and feelings of other people.

In the next four lessons you will explore the features of some forms (genres) of literary non-fiction. Some of these forms are listed below. Can you give an example of each form?

Text type	Definition
Biography	The history of someone's life written by someone else
Autobiography	An account of someone's life written by themselves
Diary	A record of daily events or experiences
Letter	A piece of writing sent to someone through the post
Travel writing	An account of a journey
Reportage	An account or story, usually found in newspapers

as a group

Complete the grid on **Worksheet 23** and be prepared to discuss your findings with the class.

Development as a group

Read the extracts on page 31 and discuss the following questions:

1 What type of text do you think each extract has been taken from? (For example, autobiography, biography, travel writing.) Give reasons for your opinion.

2 What do you learn from each of the extracts? Think about:

- Extract 1: what school life was like for the young Mandela

- Extract 2: how Ronald feels
- Extract 3: what it would be like to be in an air raid.

3 All of these texts retell or recount an event. As you may remember from your work on pages 12–13, texts that recount generally have certain features in common. Can you remember what they are? Think about:

- The order in which the events are told
- What tense they are written in
- What kind of connectives they use.

1 At Healdtown school, Nelson Mandela was a boarder and was in a dormitory which had little except beds and small lockers for each boy. He was given a mattress cover which he filled with straw to make a bed.

At 6.00 a.m. each morning a wake-up bell rang. After a quick wash in cold water, he had breakfast – a mug of hot water with sugar and a piece of bread. Lunch was the big meal and he ate lots of beans with maize porridge, sometimes with a small piece of meat. Supper was the same as breakfast. On Saturdays he could walk the seven miles to the nearest village to buy fish and chips, if he could afford it.

2

Dear Mum and Dad,

Thank you for the letter which I did not like very much. I wish you would let us come home. In this letter I am going to tell you something you have not heard before. First I am going to tell you what I have for my meals. For breakfast we have 1½ slices of bread sometimes with jam. We have a cup of tea with it. For dinner we have spuds and gravy and sometimes meat with a cup of tea. For tea we have 2 slices of bread with jam sometimes as well as a cup of tea. For supper we have one slice of bread we do not have our egg ration nor all our points or sweets. Mr Mulhary has taken my pen knife away from me because I cut myself and I don't think I'll get it back. Send another letter.

Love from Ronald
XXXXXXXXXXXX

Plenary

Feed back your findings to the class and discuss what you've learnt about literary non-fiction texts.

3

An air raid started. We all stayed in our seats after the announcement, until a thunderous crash brought us all to our feet. Then the power failed. Outside the cinema, white acrid smoke filled the street. Cries of 'Gas! Gas!' were heard. Mummy panicked and grabbed my hand as we ran this way, then that, to escape the choking fumes.

My gas-mask, in its battered box banging against my hip, never left me. I knew that the dismantled gas-mask was a sticky mess. I fumbled with it, while Mummy with her own in place was screaming weirdly through the mouth piece. She pushed me against the wall frantically trying to get my mask over my head, but the strap snapped, the thing had rotted. She shook me, slapping me about the head. Then, ripping off her own mask, she tried to force it upon me. Refusing it, I ran with her, crouching through the crowd.

Aims

In these two pages you will:

- Read extracts from different diaries and discuss the features of diary writing.
- Write a diary of your own.
- Look at an ancient recipe and explore how language changes over time.

Starter as a group

One of the diary extracts you will be looking at in this section was written in 1665 when the bubonic plague in London was at its height. The plague wiped out much of the population of many areas of Britain and Europe. You may have heard the nursery rhyme:

Ring-a-ring of roses,
A pocket full of posies,
Atishoo, atishoo,
We all fall down.

A nice little song? Actually it's a grim description of the effects of the plague. The ring of roses refers to the red rash that spread across the body of a plague victim. The posies were the bunches of herbs people carried to try to ward off the plague. Sneezing was another plague symptom. And finally, if you caught the plague you fell down – dead.

Language changes all the time. Listen carefully while your teacher reads you the recipe on **Worksheet 24**, which was written in Nottinghamshire approximately 350 years ago to help people ward off the plague.

Introduction

Diaries are one of the forms of literary non-fiction that are used to record events. People write diaries for different reasons, for example:

- As a record of thoughts and feelings
- As a record of personal events
- As a record of social events.

Often people write diaries for a combination of these reasons. As a result, diaries can provide an excellent insight into:

- A person's character
- Personal experiences
- Historical events
- Other cultures.

The diary extracts on page 33 are taken from three very different diaries. The first extract is taken from the diary of a man called Samuel Pepys (1633–1703) who lived in London during the 17th century. These entries were written in 1665 during one of the worst outbreaks of the bubonic plague in London.

The second extract is taken from the diary of Zlata Filipović, who was living in Sarajevo in Bosnia, Yugoslavia, when civil war broke out in 1992. She was eleven when she began her diary.

The third extract is taken from the diary of a Year 7 pupil, Levi.

as a class

Listen as your teacher reads each extract to you and then discuss the following questions, using **Worksheet 25** to make notes:

1. What do you think the purpose of each diary is (why has it been written)? For example, is it a record of personal or social events?

Give examples to support your opinion.

2 What do you learn from each diary extract?

3 What do you notice about the language and sentence structure used in each extract?

4 What do you learn about diary writing from these extracts?

Development on your own

Your task is to write 'The diary of a Year 7 pupil's first week at secondary school'. You can either write as yourself, or invent a fictional character and tell their story.

Remember:

- You don't have to include everything that has happened during each day; choose the important bits.
- As well as describing events, put in details about thoughts and feelings.
- You can use informal language and abbreviations but you must use correct grammar, punctuation and spelling.

1

August 12, 1665
The people die so, that now it seems they are fain to[1] carry the dead to be buried by daylight, the nights not sufficing[2] to do it in. And my Lord Mayor commands people to be within at 9 at night, all (as they say) that the sick may have liberty to go abroad for ayre.[3]

September 4, 1665
It troubled me to pass by Come Farme, where about 21 people have died of the plague and three or four days since I saw a dead corpse in a Coffin lie in the close unburyed and a watch is constantly kept there, night and day, to keep people in the plague making us cruel as dogs one to another.

September 20, 1665
But Lord, what a sad time it is, to see no boats upon the River and grass grow all and down Whitehall-court and nobody but poor wretches in the streets.

[1] have to
[2] being long enough
[3] air

Plenary

Listen to some of the diary extracts so far. Decide what sort of things need to be included to make diaries interesting to readers.

homework

Complete your diary for homework.

2

Wednesday, 20 May 1993

Dear Mimmy,
The shooting has died down. Today Mummy felt brave enough to cross the bridge. She saw Grandma and Grandad, ran into various people she knows and heard a lot of sad news. She came back all miserable. Her brother was wounded on 14 May, driving home from work. Her brother is hurt and she doesn't find out about it until today – that's terrible. He was wounded in the leg and is in hospital. How can she get to him? It's like being at the other end of the world now. They told her he's all right, but she doesn't believe them and keeps crying. If only the shooting would stop, she could go to the hospital. She says: 'I won't believe it until I see him with my own eyes.'

Zlata

3

December 4

It was freezing outside this morning and I really didn't want to get up. Mum yelled up the stairs three times before I moved. Burnt toast for breakfast, then mad dash for the bus.

Arrived at school at 9.15. Burnsy was not impressed and gave me grief for the rest of the lesson.

At lunch, Ravi showed me the trainers he got for his b'day. They're Nike and they're completely wicked. Must ask mum and dad to get me some for Xmas.

The afternoon was just as deadly as the morning: double games in the rain. Had to walk home soaking wet. Mum and Ben were rowing when I got home, so I scarpered upstairs. Today has been a real hassle, I'm very glad to be in bed!

Biographies and autobiographies

Aims

In these two pages you will:

● Explore the features of autobiographies and biographies.

● Revise similar spellings for the sound 'oo'.

Starter on your own

1 Look at the poem on **Worksheet 26**, which is full of different 'oo' sounds. There are several different ways of spelling this sound in English: the worksheet will help you identify these spellings.

2 Now look at the 20 words below. In groups, pronounce these words carefully and see if you can work out a rule for when c is pronounced softly (like an s) and when it is hard (like a k).

cat	resources	decide
cent	necessary	success
cinema	receive	physical
cot	caught	participation
cut	column	acid
science	alcohol	circumference
conscious	audience	

3 Pretend you are going to explain this rule to a much younger child, using the words listed above to illustrate your point. How would you group the words and what would you say to explain the rule?

To help you sort the words into groups, you will be provided with them separately on cards (**Worksheet 27**).

 Look at the words in your spelling log and see if this rule helps.

Introduction as a class

Two other forms of literary non-fiction are autobiographies and biographies. As you will remember from the work you did on page 30, an autobiography is an account of a person's life told by themselves and a biography is an account of a person's life told by someone else. As with diaries, autobiographies and biographies can give an insight into the lives of other people.

The extract on page 35 is taken from Floella Benjamin's autobiography, *Coming to England*, in which she describes emigrating to England from Trinidad in the early 1960s. In this extract, Floella describes what the weather was like on the island of Trinidad. Listen as your teacher reads the extract and then discuss the following points.

1 What do you learn about the weather in Trinidad in this description?

2 What are Floella Benjamin's feelings towards the weather in the first two paragraphs? How can you tell? Think about the way she describes it, as well as her actions and thoughts.

3 What scares Floella about the unusual weather in the third paragraph?

4 The passage includes lots of descriptions. Find as many descriptive words as you can.

5 Is the passage written in informal or formal language?

6 What is the narrative voice of the passage?

There were usually two kinds of weather on our tropical island, which was not far from the equator: hot or rainy. When it was hot, from December to June, it was very hot. In the mornings we would wake to brilliant blue cloudless skies with a bright yellow sun beating down on us. The only relief was the occasional cool breeze that drifted in from the sea. You couldn't move fast in the heat, so everything was done at a slow pace. You could feel the heat through the soles of your feet as you walked along. People would often stop and stand idly on street corners chatting while they wiped away the sweat …

I loved the sun because the heat warmed my inner soul and gave me a free, happy, relaxed feeling. I also got a good feeling when it rained – and when it rained, it *really* rained. The heavens would open and torrents of rain would lash down. We would dance and splash in the warm, tropical, scented water. It didn't matter if we got wet because, after the downpour, the water would evaporate in no time, drying our clothes in an instant …

One day I remember experiencing weather like I had never seen before. One minute there was brilliant sunshine, the next a great darkness enveloped the island. At the same time the ground trembled, causing cracks to appear under my feet. A waterpipe erupted, flooding the main street. I really thought the world was going to end and I screamed for my mother in terror. She told me it was freak weather, an eclipse and a slight earthquake happening, amazingly, at the same time. She held me tight and told me that it wouldn't last long. I was only seven years old and I didn't fully understand at the time what was happening. All I knew was that my little world looked and felt different. Then an almighty downpour of rain started to fall and for once I didn't dance in it.

Development *in pairs*

The second extract, on **Worksheet 28**, is taken from a biography of a 13-year-old girl, Anne Frank. During the Second World War, Anne and her family hid from the Nazis for two years in an apartment block in Amsterdam. In this extract we learn what their refuge was like when they first arrived. Listen as your teacher reads it to you and then in pairs discuss the following questions, annotating the extract on the worksheet.

1 What do you learn about Anne's hiding place?

2 What clues can you find in the text about Anne's character? Underline examples on your worksheet.

3 What descriptive language does the passage contain? Underline examples in a different colour on your worksheet.

4 Is it written in formal or informal language?

5 What is the narrative voice of the passage?

Plenary

Draw up a short table like the one below listing the similarities and differences between the way autobiographies and biographies are written. Be prepared to share these points in a class discussion.

Similarities	Differences

Consolidation

Aims

In these two pages you will:

- Review all the work you have done on literary non-fiction by writing a story in three different genres.
- Review how the magic 'e' helps you to spell words, and work out a rule for spelling words with soft and hard 'c'.

Starter *as a group*

At primary school you may have been taught the 'magic e', which is probably the most useful spelling rule in English. It's all about the difference that adding an 'e' onto a **consonant-vowel-consonant** (CVC) word (such as 'fat') makes to the sound. The short 'a' sound of 'fat' is transformed into the long 'a' sound of 'fate'. In other words, the addition of the 'e' makes the vowel say its own name. It works for all five vowels. This remains true for CCVC words, as well, for example 'plan' becomes 'plane'.

Look what happens when you want to add 'ing' to these words. 'Plan' becomes 'planning' and 'plane' becomes 'planing'. Doubling the last consonant keeps the 'a' sound short, while deleting the 'e' and adding any suffix beginning with a vowel keeps the vowel sound long.

Your group will be given a number of cards with words on that could be used to illustrate this rule, plus the five vowels (**Worksheet 29**). Your task is to see if you can work out a good way of using these cards to help an eight-year-old child understand the magic e rule. See what ideas you can come up with.

consonant any letter other than the vowels
vowel any of the letters 'a', 'e', 'i', 'o' or 'u'

Introduction *on your own*

In this lesson you will revise all the work you've done on literary non-fiction by writing an extract from a diary, a biography and an autobiography.

First think about an event in your life when you got into trouble for something or felt really embarrassed, for example:

- You broke something valuable.
- You got caught doing something wrong.
- You were forced to wear something you didn't want to wear.

Brainstorm all your thoughts about what happened and how you felt on **Worksheet 30**, using a spider diagram like the one below.

Setting: sitting-room

Event: breaking a window

How I felt: I was so shocked I thought I would be sick

What happened: I was playing football indoors …

Development *on your own*

You are now going to use the information from your spider diagram in your own writing. You may not want to include all the details about your event in each of the activities below, so select what you use carefully.

1 Write about your event as if it was an extract in your *diary*. Remember that diaries:

- Often focus on the main events, rather than describing the small details
- Indicate how you are feeling
- Can include abbreviations
- Can include informal language
- Are written in the first person
- Are usually written in the past tense.

2 Now write about the event as if it was an extract from your *autobiography*. Remember that autobiographies:

- Describe the events in detail, using descriptive language
- Indicate how you were feeling at the time
- Use Standard English
- Are written in the first person
- Are written in the past tense.

3 Swap your autobiography with a partner's. Imagine that you are your partner's biographer, and write about the same event as an extract from a *biography*. Remember that biographies:

- Describe the events in detail, using descriptive language
- Suggest how someone might be feeling by how they behave
- Use Standard English
- Are written in the third person
- Are written in the past tense.

> **!** **Remember** to read your work through carefully, correcting any errors and redrafting sentences that could be improved. Finish with a brief comment summing up how well you think you have completed the task.

Plenary

Think about your diary, autobiography and biography. Which was the easiest piece to write? Which was the most challenging? Why?

Share your views in a class discussion.

In this section you have learnt how to imagine, explore and entertain by reading and writing more effectively in a wide range of narrative and recount styles.

In particular, you've explored:

- How effective stories are structured
- How narrative devices are used by authors to make their writing enjoyable
- How descriptive language can be used to create an effective setting
- How characters can be portrayed through their actions, effective description and dialogue
- How to recognize the key features of some forms of literary non-fiction, including diaries, biographies and autobiographies.

You have shown your grasp of these skills by planning and writing your own short story and by writing a story in three different genres.

Reflect on what you've learnt from this section and then, in your exercise book, write targets to improve your work. You should consider the following areas:

- Spelling
- Vocabulary
- Sentence structure
- Planning your writing
- Reading
- Speaking and listening.

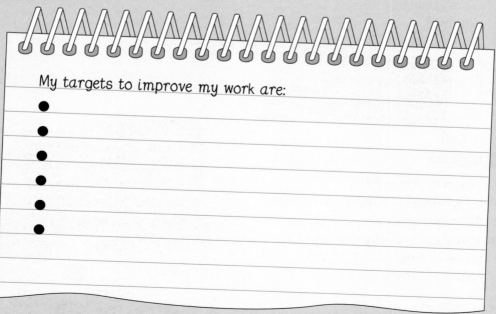

My targets to improve my work are:

-
-
-
-
-
-

Inform, explain, describe

Introduction

Have you ever tried to inform a grandparent about your latest computer game? Or explain to him or her how it works? Or describe, perhaps in a letter, the characters that appear on the screen?

There are so many texts that provide incredible information and detailed explanations and descriptions, it is important that you are familiar with the kind of language that they use. If you are writing these texts yourself, it is essential that you are able to use the right type of language in order to convey your ideas clearly.

Key aim

In this section you will:

- Develop your own skills in reading and writing information and explanation texts, including how to make description effective.

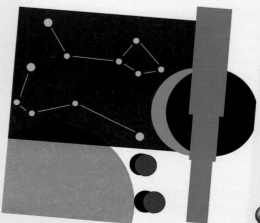

Texts for different purposes

Aims

On these two pages you will:
- Revisit writing for information and explanation.
- Explore the features of each type of writing.
- Understand that the purpose of a text influences the way it is written.

Starter  as a group

You need to be in groups of three for this activity (**Worksheet 31**).

- Each person will be given a number – 1, 2 or 3.
- Every group will be given a card which lists three tasks.
- The person numbered 1 will complete task 1, the person numbered 2 task 2 etc.
- You have only one minute each to complete your task.
- When you have finished the group will have three minutes to discuss the final question on the card.
- Be ready to feed back your answers to the class.

Introduction

You will remember from your literacy work in previous years that:

- An *information* text describes and organizes facts so that people can easily discover all that they require. It often begins with a general classification. The writing should be structured carefully, in a logical order, giving examples, names, dates etc. where necessary. This type of text should be written in an **impersonal** way, and in the present tense whenever it is appropriate. Encyclopaedias, dictionaries and guide books are examples of information texts.

- An *explanation* text gives details about how or why something happens. This type of text should develop ideas logically, step by step, clearly showing the link between what causes something to happen and the effect it creates. It is also usually impersonal and written in the present tense. Scientific, geographical and historical writing often gives explanations for processes or events.

Both of these types of text, as well as many others, depend on clear *descriptive* writing for their success. Describing things accurately and in a way that helps the reader to picture them is an important part of writing non-fiction, as well as fiction (see pages 20–35). Adjectives and imagery, such as similes and metaphors, can help to make descriptive writing more effective.

> **impersonal** writing that uses the third person (he, she or it) is described as impersonal; 'I' is not used

Development as a group

Working in small groups of three or four, examine each of the short extracts on this page. For each one say:

1 What the writing is about. Give a sentence of no more than ten words to summarize its *content*.

2 What the *purpose* of the writing is. Is it to describe, or to inform, or to explain?

3 How you know what *type* of writing it is. Give examples, using quotations from the text. (Use the definitions on page 40 to help you.)

1

A <u>lunar</u>[1] eclipse can occur only at the time of a Full Moon – that is, when the Moon is on the side of the Earth opposite to that of the Sun … When the Moon moves through the shadow of the Earth, it loses its bright direct illumination by the Sun, although its disk still remains faintly visible … After a part of the Moon's surface is in the <u>umbra</u>[2] and thus darkened, the Moon is said to be in partial eclipse. After about an hour, when the whole disk of the Moon is within the umbra, the eclipse becomes total. If the Moon's path leads through the centre of the umbra, the total eclipse can be expected to last about an hour and three-quarters.

[1] *of the moon*
[2] *region of shadow*

2

Thickets of alder, black poplar and cypress, with horned owls and falcons, and <u>garrulous</u>[1] sea-crows roosting in their branches, sheltered Calypso's great cavern. A grape-vine twisted across the entrance. Parsley and irises grew thick in an adjoining meadow, which was fed by four clear streams. Here lovely Calypso welcomed Odysseus as he stumbled ashore.

[1] *chattering*

3

Odysseus: In Greek mythology, one of the foremost of the Greek heroes at the siege of Troy, noted for his courage and <u>ingenuity</u>.[1] His return to his kingdom of Ithaca was <u>fraught</u>[2] with adventures in which he lost all his companions, and he was acknowledged by his wife Penelope only after killing her <u>suitors</u>.[3] Roman name: **Ulysses**.

[1] *cleverness*
[2] *filled*
[3] *men who wanted to marry her*

Plenary

Feed back your answers to questions 1–3 to the class by annotating an enlarged copy of the text for display in the classroom (**Worksheet 32**). Make sure that some key features of the types of text have been identified, as well as how description is used in each type.

homework

Write about the features of each of the three texts you have studied in the lesson, describing their content, purpose and type.

> **!** ***Remember*** to read your work carefully, improve it if necessary, and write a brief comment on how well you think you have completed the task.

Creating impressive description

Aims

On these two pages you will:

- Read a text closely to find the information you need.
- Examine how a writer can create a vivid description using adjectives and imagery.
- Increase your understanding of some of the devices that a writer can use to describe objects and events.
- Demonstrate your understanding of how to create an accurate description that stays with the reader.
- Distinguish between the everyday uses of some words and their more technical meaning.

Starter

When you want to describe something, the most important thing is to select exactly the right word that sums up what is being described. However, many words have a variety of different meanings. Even more confusing, many words also have an additional meaning when used in a particular technical context, which is much more precise than the meaning they have in everyday use. Take the word 'mass', for example:

- In RE, mass is a Christian religious service.
- In science, mass is the amount of matter that an object has, measured in grams.
- In everyday use, mass is a large amount of something.

Your teacher will provide you with some cards on which there are words with both a general and a technical, specific meaning, like mass (**Worksheet 33**). Your task is to match up each word with its technical definition, and then come up with a sentence using it in its everyday context.

Introduction

About 2,800 years ago Homer, a poet from ancient Greece, was telling stories based on the **myths** of his people. It is amazing to think that, not only do people still read his work today, but also so much of our own literature and culture is based on the stories that he told.

The passage on page 43 is adapted from one of Homer's most loved works, a huge poem called *The Odyssey*. It tells the story of Odysseus, a Greek hero returning home from the Trojan wars.

This short extract is a good example of Homer's powers of description. Look in particular at the section describing the storm that the angry Poseidon stirred up against defenceless Odysseus. The winds are personifications of angry figures, stirring up the sea in their violent attack.

> **myth** an ancient story of gods or heroes which attempts to explain events or human nature

1 Examine the whole passage to find evidence of how Homer makes his description dramatic for the reader. Remind yourself of the work you did on pages 20–21 and then look for at least one example of each of the following:

- Adjectives
- Powerful verbs
- Similes
- Metaphors or personification.

2 What else has Homer done to make his description sound interesting, for example the use of exaggeration or impressive vocabulary?

Development *on your own*

Use the descriptive devices listed in question 1 above to write a paragraph that describes an old man walking home from the shops on a stormy evening in winter.

! **Remember** to read your work carefully, improve it if necessary, and write a brief comment on how well you think you have completed the task.

Plenary

Three members of the class will be asked to read out their paragraphs.

- Listen carefully and see if you can identify the adjectives and similes they have included.
- Has anyone managed to use any personification?

On his way home from Troy Odysseus lingered for many years with the goddess Calypso, who wanted him to stay with her forever. However, Odysseus grew increasingly homesick. Eventually he decided to risk the wrath of the god Poseidon, whose territory he had to cross, and make his way back to his homeland.

It was with a happy heart that Odysseus spread his sail to catch the wind and used his seamanship to keep his boat straight with the steering-oar. There he sat and never closed his eyes in sleep, but watched the stars slowly set, especially the Great Bear, which looks across at Orion the Hunter with a wary eye. It was this constellation,[1] the only one which never bathes in Ocean's Stream,[2] that the wise goddess Calypso had told him to keep on his left hand as he made across the sea.

For seventeen days he sailed on his course, and on the eighteenth there came into sight the shadowy mountains of the Phaeacians' country, which jutted out to meet him there. The land looked like a shield laid on the misty sea. But now Poseidon,[3] Lord of the Earthquake, observed him from the distant mountains. The sight of Odysseus sailing over the seas added fresh fuel to his anger. He shook his head and muttered to himself: 'I mean to let him have his bellyful of trouble yet.'

Whereupon he marshalled[4] the clouds and seizing his trident[5] in his hands stirred up the sea. He roused the stormy blasts of every wind that blows, and covered land and water alike with a canopy[6] of cloud. Darkness swooped down from the sky. East Wind and South and the tempestuous West fell to on one another, and from the North came a white squall,[7] rolling a great wave in its van.[8] Odysseus' knees shook and his spirit quailed.

A mountainous wave, advancing with majestic sweep, crashed down upon him from above and whirled his vessel round. The steering-oar was torn from his hands, and he himself was tossed off the boat, while at the same moment the warring winds joined forces in one tremendous gust, which snapped the mast in two and flung the sail and yard-arm far out into the sea.

From Homer, *The Odyssey*, Book 5

[1] group of stars
[2] the circle of water that surrounded the Earth, according to the Greeks
[3] mythological god of the sea and earthquakes, usually portrayed holding a trident; also known as Neptune
[4] gathered together
[5] three-pronged spear
[6] an awning, cover
[7] sudden wind or storm
[8] in front

Aims

On these two pages you will:

- Revisit information and reference texts and alphabetical order.
- Evaluate and compare different types of texts.
- Practise using the dictionary quickly and with skill to find words that begin with the same letter or letters.
- Use the information you have gained to write on your own.

Starter *as a group*

1 The class will be divided into two teams, and each team will be given a number of words (**Worksheet 34**).

2 The team has up to five minutes to put the words they have been given into alphabetical order. (Remember: when words begin with the same letter, they are placed in order according to their *second* letter. Discuss how you would place in order words that begin with the same *two* letters.)

3 Think about how to make best use of all the members of your team.

4 The first team to finish correctly, or to have the most words in order in the given time, wins. The winning group will explain the process they used.

Introduction *on your own*

1 Refresh your memory by reading Box 1 below about information and reference texts.

2 Now read Box 2, which is an example of a short information text.

as a class

As a class, talk about the text in Box 2:

- Where might this type of information be found?
- How many facts are given here?
- What information is missing that you might also like to know?

1

Information and **reference** texts provide people with a wealth of facts, details and data. Encyclopaedias and dictionaries are perhaps the most common and popular texts that people use for researching information, but even these come in many different forms: there are specialist dictionaries for scientists and linguists, and encyclopaedias dedicated only to literature and history.

Nowadays we can also gather information from a much wider variety of different sources – not just books, but also CD-ROMs, the internet, television ceefax pages, the telephone, leaflets etc.

In order to help people find information quickly, the text needs to be organized in a way that is helpful to the researcher. This may include alphabetical order, chapter headings or an index at the back of the book.

2

Ovid (43 BC–AD 17) was a famous poet from the ancient world. He was a Roman and he wrote in Latin. His greatest work, the *Metamorphoses*, is a poem in 15 books telling mythological and historical tales. One of the tales he tells is about the young lovers Pyramus and Thisbe. Many centuries later the famous English dramatist William Shakespeare (1564–1616) used Ovid's story as part of his play *A Midsummer Night's Dream* and as an inspiration for *Romeo and Juliet*.

Development

One of the things in Box 2 that you might want to know more about is the story of Pyramus and Thisbe. An ordinary dictionary or encyclopaedia might not be very helpful, so it would be better to use a specialist source. A good example would be a dictionary of classical mythology. The extract opposite is taken from such a dictionary.

as a group

In order to fully understand the nature of information texts you must examine their language and expression. In small groups, discuss the following questions and make notes that you can refer to later.

1 List the language clues that tell us that the extract is an information or reference text, not a story told by a skilled storyteller. For example: layout, sentence structure, vocabulary and so on. Why do you think this extract is in the past tense?

2 Compare this passage with the way Homer told his story in the previous lesson (page 43). What is missing from this text, that Homer used so skilfully? Support your response with examples.

3 Evaluate this text. What is its purpose? How does the purpose affect the way in which the information is given and the language that is used? Is it successful? Explain your reasons.

> **Pyramus and Thisbe.** Young Assyrian[1] lovers. Pyramus and Thisbe grew up in adjoining houses and fell in love, but were not allowed by their families to marry one another. After long nights of whispering through a chink in the wall between their houses, they determined to meet at night at the tomb of King Ninus. Thisbe arrived first, but was frightened away by a lioness, which then mauled with its bloody jaws the cloak that Thisbe had dropped. Pyramus, on finding the cloak, thought himself responsible for his loved one's death and killed himself with his sword. His blood changed the blooms and fruit of the mulberry tree, beneath which he fell, from their former[2] white to purple. Thisbe returned and, discovering Pyramus' body, killed herself with the same sword. The ashes of the unfortunate pair were buried in the same urn by their parents. [Ovid, *Metamorphoses*, 4.55–166.]

[1] from Assyria (ancient Iraq)
[2] previous

Plenary

On your whiteboards or a piece of paper, write down three important things that you have learnt this lesson about information and reference texts. When you are ready, hold them above your head.

homework

Re-tell part of the story of Pyramus and Thisbe in the style of Homer.
Hints:
- Make it sound like a story, not a dictionary entry.
- Include description.

> **!** **Remember** to read your work carefully, improve it if necessary, and write a brief comment on how well you think you have completed the task.

Making an explanation clear

Aims

On these two pages you will:
- Revise instructions.
- Learn the difference between instructions and explanations.
- Demonstrate that you can identify the features of an explanation text.
- Write an explanation of your own.
- Identify the features of spoken directions.

Starter

Imagine that you have to give directions to a new visitor to your school. Your teacher will tell you where they need to be directed to. In pairs, take it in turns to give each other directions.

as a class

Now, as a class, discuss what problems you found you had with giving the directions. What do you think you need to remember about the following points when giving directions:
- Audience
- Structure
- Language
- Tone?

Remind yourself of the work you did on writing instructions on pages 10–11. What were the ingredients of good instruction writing? (Look at **Worksheet 35** if you need to jog your memory.) Do you think these ingredients are important in giving good spoken directions? What are the main differences between written instructions and spoken directions?

Introduction

There are many similarities between instructions and explanations, but the important difference between them is that:
- *Instructions tell you how to make or do something*: examples are a recipe for a pudding, or a manual telling you how to set up and play a computer game.
- *Explanations tell you why or how something happens*, showing a relationship between cause and effect, such as why yeast makes bread rise or how electricity is created.

You will remember from your work in previous years that an explanation text usually:
- Includes a series of logical steps explaining how or why something occurs
- Helps the reader to make *links* between points
- Shows how one thing can *connect* with another to *cause* something to happen
- Is written in the present tense
- Uses the more formal impersonal voice of the third person (s/he, it, they)
- Often has diagrams to give the reader a picture of what is happening.

In the example on page 47 the writer is *explaining how* air movement in the Earth's atmosphere *causes* rain to fall. An essential element of an explanation text, such as this one, is that it should explain in a logical way the links between the events that are being described.

1 Study the text by yourself and see if you can clearly identify the process that is being explained.

in pairs

2 Study the text in pairs and then explain to each other, in your own words, what causes air to rise and fall in the atmosphere. Listen to each other carefully and make sure that you can fully understand what your partner is saying.

3 Now fill in **Worksheet 36**, which asks you to identify various important features of explanation texts.

Development *on your own*

Your task is to write a very simple explanation of the water cycle for a class of eight-year-olds, using the bulleted information below to help you.

■ Water evaporates from oceans, lakes, rivers and plants when heated by the sun.

■ It condenses to form clouds.

■ Clouds release their water back to the land as rain, hail, dew or snow.

■ Water runs into rivers and streams and flows back to the oceans.

Support your text with clear, simple diagrams. If you think any of the words you use are too difficult for eight-year-olds, use a dictionary to help you provide a simple explanation for them.

Plenary

Check your partner's explanation – is it:

• Clear, making connections between points

• Impersonal (using s/he it, they)

• In the present tense?

AIR MOVEMENT

THE EARTH'S <u>atmosphere</u>[1] is made up of gases. <u>Gravity</u>[2] forces these gases downwards, so that the atmosphere is most <u>dense</u>[3] at the earth's surface. Cold air is more dense than warm air, so it sinks, creating areas of high <u>pressure</u>.[4] Warm air rises, leaving behind areas of low pressure.

These air movements lead to changes in the weather. For example, when moist, warm air rises and cools, water <u>vapour</u>[5] within it condenses to form clouds, and sometimes rain.

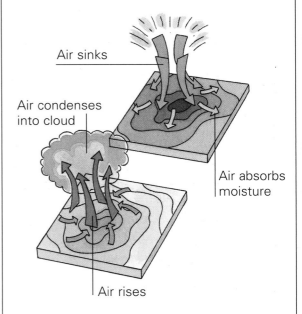

Air sinks

Air condenses into cloud

Air absorbs moisture

Air rises

High and low pressure
Cold air sinks, creating high pressure, which often brings fine weather. Warm air rises, creating low pressure, which may bring coldness or rain.

---

[1] *the air around us*
[2] *the force that pulls objects to the centre of the Earth*
[3] *solid*
[4] *force or weight*
[5] *steam or mist which sometimes cannot be seen*

Information and sources

Aims

On these two pages you will:

- Discover that information can be found in a variety of different types of places and forms.
- Develop your skills in researching reference texts for information.
- Make decisions about when it is appropriate to use these different sources.
- Learn to acknowledge where your information has come from.

Starter

When looking for information, knowing what reference book to use is half the battle. If you wanted to look up which countries are neighbours of Turkey, you would need an atlas (a book of maps). Your teacher will give you the following three types of information cut up on separate cards (**Worksheet 37**):

- Questions
- Definitions of different reference books
- The name given to these reference books.

Your task is to sort the information into three columns as follows:

Question	Name of suitable reference text	The type of information it contains
Which countries are neighbours of Turkey?	Atlas	A book of maps

Introduction

Nowadays electronic devices such as computers, television, radio and the telephone all help to provide us with information. Some people say finding things out has never been easier, others say it is more difficult because we have too many choices. What do you think?

as a group

1 Your teacher will divide the class into five groups. Each group should consider one of the five types of information storage listed on **Worksheet 38**. Use the planning frame provided to record your ideas.

as a class

2 Report back and take a whole class vote. What do you think?

Development in pairs

The greatest problem facing anyone searching reference texts for information is the vast range of material they may have to sort through.

The following numbered points in bold are key to successful research. Your teacher will explain these to you and ask key questions to help you develop these skills.

1 **Know exactly what it is you want to find out before you start.**

Pretend you are in a citizenship lesson studying the right to roam (the history behind people's right to walk freely throughout certain parts of the country). Your teacher has set the following research homework: 'Find out what the event in 1932 called the Kinder Trespass was and why it happened.'

What is the question asking?

2 Think carefully about where you would be most likely to find the information you are looking for.

Where could you look for this information?

Imagine you've managed to find a book called *The 1932 Kinder Trespass*. But until you've looked at it you can't be sure if it will be useful.

3 Read quickly (skimming or scanning) to find the information you need.

What do the terms 'skimming' and 'scanning' mean?

You will find the first five paragraphs of chapter 1 of *The 1932 Kinder Trespass* on **Worksheet 39**. Skim the paragraphs and decide if it is useful. Scan the passage to see if it suggests any causes of the trespass.

4 Evaluate what you find and decide whether it is useful.

Do you think this passage will be useful in answering the question?

5 Make notes on what is helpful.

What does making notes involve?

As you know, all you have to find out is:

● What the trespass was
● What might have caused it.

See if you can jot down notes on these two topics in a few words.

6 Be prepared to ignore what you don't need.

Why is this important?

Look back at the passage and at your notes and decide which paragraphs or sentences were the basis for your notes.

Approximately what percentage of the passage does this equal?

7 Make a note of the source of your information (title and author of the reference text) to use as an acknowledgement.

Why is this important?

Where might the source information be found?

Plenary

When you need to research some information what must you remember to do? Each person should think of one point.

Students researching in the library.

Information and instructions

Aims

On these two pages you will:

- Learn that order and organization are important when giving information.
- Understand that the opening sentences of paragraphs should signal the topic that they concern.
- Organize and write an information text yourself.
- Analyse how punctuation helps to make your writing clearer.

Starter

Punctuation helps to make whatever you are writing clear. Sometimes, if punctuation has been forgotten or used incorrectly, people may misunderstand what is being said.

> **punctuation** a way of marking text with symbols (punctuation marks) to help readers' understanding. The most common punctuation marks are: apostrophe, bracket, colon, comma, dash, exclamation mark, full stop, hyphen, inverted comma (speech mark), question mark and semi-colon.

in pairs

1 Read the passage on **Worksheet 40**.
2 Highlight all the punctuation marks that the writer has used.
3 Make a list of all the different types of punctuation marks that you know.
4 Ask about any that you don't recognize.
5 Find examples of the following types of commas and circle them in red on the sheet:
   - commas that are used to mark off words in a list
   - commas that are used to mark off extra information attached to a sentence
   - commas that are used to mark a short pause in a sentence.

as a class

1 How do these commas help us to understand what the writer is saying?
2 What would happen if all the punctuation marks were removed?

Introduction

Human beings have been gathering information for a very long time. In order for other people to make sense of this information it has to be written in a particular way. For example, information texts are usually:

- Organized in the order that suits the purpose (chronological, logical, alphabetical, importance etc.)
- Written in the present tense
- Written in the third person (s/he, it, they)
- Stored in many ways for others to use.

as a group

1 **Worksheet 41** contains an information text about Saturn. Read the text together. You will have noticed that there is something wrong with this text. The paragraphs have been deliberately mixed up so that they are not in a logical order. Arrange the paragraphs into a more logical order. Then answer these questions:

- Why is the first sentence of each paragraph important? What does it do?
- What are the reasons for the order you have chosen?

2 Demonstrate your knowledge of the features of an information text by filling in the grid on **Worksheet 42** with examples from the text on Saturn.

Development *on your own*

On the right is some information about the planet Pluto. It has been presented in a table, but it is not very well organized. Your task is to use the information in the table to write three paragraphs about Pluto, as an entry for a scientific encyclopaedia that specializes in information about the solar system.

Remember that when you are writing an information text you should:

Information about the planet Pluto	
Diameter at the Equator	2,290 km
Existence first detected	1930
Time taken to orbit the Sun	248.54 years
Distance from the Sun in relation to other planets	The furthest
Number of moons	1
Composition	Rocky core, covering of ice
Speed of orbit around the Sun	4.74 km per second
Atmosphere	methane
Time taken for one rotation on its axis	6.39 days
Size in relation to other planets	Smallest in our solar system
Name of Pluto's moon	Charon
Average distance from the Sun	5.91 billion km
First detected by	Clyde Tombaugh

Dorling Kindersley Encyclopedia of Science

- Choose the information you wish to include – you don't have to include everything.
- Organize the points and link them together in a logical order (put things together that go together).
- Make sure that the first sentence of every paragraph informs the reader of the topic that the paragraph will cover.
- Use the present tense and the third person.
- Use punctuation, such as commas, to help make your information clear.

> **!** **Remember** to read your work carefully, correcting any errors and redrafting sentences that could be improved. Finish with a brief comment summing up how well you think you have completed the task.

Plenary

Exchange your writing on Pluto with a partner's. Read through each other's work. Discuss how well you have done by matching the writing against the features listed in the bullet points above.

Make a note of anything you have forgotten to do, or not done very well, so you can remember to focus on this next time.

Aims

On these two pages you will:

- Discuss and plan your own inquiry, using your investigation skills to inform, explain and describe.
- Revise descriptive writing.
- Understand the difference between a fact and an opinion.

Starter

Descriptive writing plays an important part in helping us to 'see' the real or imaginary world around us.

on your own

Look at **Worksheet 43**, which describes the planet Mars. Highlight the parts that add to the descriptive power of the passage, by using adjectives, adverbs, effective nouns and verbs and imagery such as metaphors or similes.

in pairs

1 Compare the pieces that you have highlighted – are they the same?

2 Find an example of something which you consider to be a **fact**.

3 Find an example of something which you consider to be an **opinion**.

4 What is the difference between a fact and an opinion?

Keep the sheet – it may come in useful later on.

> **fact** a piece of information which is true
> **opinion** a belief or view about someone or something

Introduction *as a class*

For many hundreds of years people have imagined what it would be like to find other forms of life in our universe. So far, all we have learnt about the planets suggests that, unlike Earth, they are not very hospitable places for human life, or life of any kind.

Patrick Moore, a famous English astronomer, thinks that Mars is the only possible place in our universe able to support life – as long as we put it there ourselves. Read what he says (top of page 53).

Development *as a group*

Is Patrick Moore right? Can you imagine that people would settle on Mars, knowing that they and their children could never return to Earth? What would life on this alien planet be like?

The planet Mars

In order to give informed answers to these questions, you will first need to do some talking, thinking and research. Follow the instructions on page 53 carefully. These will form the basis of your research in the next lesson (pages 54–55).

Could human beings live on Mars?

Tourism to Mars may come eventually, though certainly not until well into the twenty-first century. There will also be children born and brought up on Mars, and this brings me to another point which I have seldom seen stressed elsewhere. Will a boy or girl born and reared on Mars ever be able to come to Earth, where the pull of gravity is much greater? Imagine how you would feel if, without any increase in your muscle power or your heart strength, your weight suddenly increased by a factor of three. You might not be able to cope. I am prepared to believe that within the next hundred years there may be two entirely separate branches of <u>Homo sapiens</u>:[1] Earth-<u>dwellers</u>,[2] and our <u>kinsfolk</u>[3] from Mars who can never come to Earth at all, though naturally they would be quite happy on the moon. This may sound like science fiction in 1998, but by 2098 it may have become science fact.

Patrick Moore

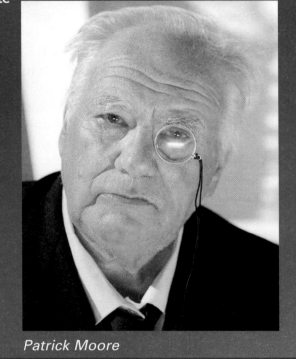

Patrick Moore

[1] the scientific name given to human beings
[2] residents, people who live in a particular place
[3] people we are distantly related to

1 First form groups of four or five.

2 Then spend ten minutes discussing your opinions on the subject of life on Mars. Would it be possible for people to live on Mars, as Patrick Moore suggests? Use **Worksheet 44** to jot down your ideas.

3 Next, draw up a list of points and ideas under the headings:
   - Reasons why people might want to live on Mars
   - Reasons why it might be difficult to live on Mars.

4 Then pool the knowledge of the group – what facts do you already know, or think you know, about the planet Mars?

5 Finally, prepare a list of questions – information you need to find out about Mars, in order to make a better, more informed, response to the question of whether human beings could live on Mars.

Plenary

Each group will be asked to give feedback about how it plans to work in the next lesson. What information are you hoping to find? What descriptions and explanations will you need to make to support your point of view?

Living on Mars: research

Aims

On these two pages you will:

- Use a variety of reference texts and research skills to conduct your research.
- Identify and practise different ways of working out the meaning of unknown words.

Starter  in pairs

People who study the solar system, like Patrick Moore, are called astronomers. An etymological dictionary, which explains the origins of words, tells us that the stem or word root 'astro' comes from the Greek word for 'star'. Knowing the origins of words is one way of helping you to understand the meaning of words that you don't recognize. Some other useful ways of trying to understand what a word means are by:

- Looking at the context – (the rest of the sentence or passage may give you some clues).
- Thinking of other similar words that you know – your new word may have the same word root, for example telescope, television, telephone all have the same root 'tele' from ancient Greek, meaning 'far off'.
- Listen to the sound – some words are onomatopoeic, so the sound of the word is related to its meaning, for example, crack, splash, hiss.

Working with your partner read the passage opposite, which describes a piece of rock (a meteorite) found on Earth, which is believed to have come from Mars 13,000 years ago. It is an example of the type of information text that you may come across in your own research. Record your knowledge of the ten words that have been underlined in the appropriate columns on **Worksheet 45**.

The rock in the meteorite has been age-dated to about 4.5 billion years, the period when the planet Mars formed. The rock is extensively fractured by impacts as meteorites bombarded the planets in the solar system. Between 3.6 billion and 4 billion years ago water is believed to have penetrated fractures in the subsurface rock, possibly forming an underground water system.

Because the water was saturated with carbon dioxide from the Martian atmosphere, carbonate minerals were deposited in the fractures. The team's findings indicate living organisms may also have helped in the formation of the carbonate, and some remains of the microscopic organisms may have become fossilized. Then, 15 million years ago, a huge comet or asteroid struck Mars, ejecting a piece of the rock with enough force to escape the planet. For millions of years, the chunk of rock floated through space. It encountered Earth's atmosphere 13,000 years ago and fell in Antarctica as a meteorite.

Introduction as a group

In this lesson you will begin the research on the planet Mars that you planned in the last lesson (pages 52–53). In the next lesson (pages 56–57) you will use the information that you have researched to explain and support your views, by preparing and giving a presentation to the class about the possibility of people living on Mars in 2098.

Think back to other work that you have completed in this section. Once you have found an appropriate text for your research, what should you do to extract the information and make the most effective use of your time? In your groups, write down three helpful hints to guide the successful researcher.

The research box below will remind you of some of the other things you will need to remember.

Research

⊙ Use *different types of sources*, and choose the most appropriate ones that will best answer each of the questions you developed last lesson (page 53).

⊙ Note all the titles and authors of the sources you use, so that you can list your *acknowledgements* in your presentation.

⊙ Use *short **quotations** and technical words* from the original source, but the rest must be in your own words.

⊙ Apply your *word skills* from the starter activity or use a *dictionary* to help you find out the meanings of new or difficult words.

⊙ A *thesaurus* will help you to avoid repeating a word or to think of similar words to avoid copying those used in your source material.

Note: Every member of the group must make a contribution to the research and the presentation.

quotation a phrase or passage that is repeated in another text to give evidence of something or to support a particular view. Short quotations are usually put inside inverted commas in the main body of the text; longer quotations are usually set off from the text, with a space above and below, and don't use inverted commas.

Now make a grid like the one below, based on the questions you developed in the last lesson to help you focus your research.

| What are the conditions on Mars? | Mars is ... |

Development *as a group*

In your groups discuss what you have each discovered through your research. Use the information to help you to talk about your opinions. Now organize your findings in a way that will help you to answer the question: Could human beings live on Mars? Use the grid on **Worksheet 46** to help you.

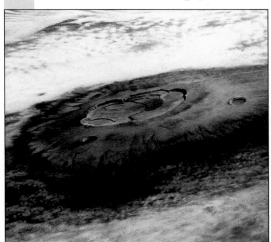

Plenary   *The surface of Mars*

How could you judge whether or not your research was successful? What do you need to do if you have not yet found enough useful information?

Living on Mars: presentation

7 The Martians ordered the astronauts to get into their spaceship.

8 It was Neil Armstrong what was the first man on the Moon.

pronoun a word used to replace a noun, a noun phrase or a clause, in order to avoid repetition

Aims

On these two pages you will:

- Revise and use the skills you have gained to inform, explain and describe in the presentation you are preparing in your group.
- Work together as a group to give a presentation to the rest of the class.
- Evaluate how well you and others have done.
- Increase your understanding that using pronouns incorrectly can make sentences confusing.

Starter  in pairs

Look at the sentences below.

- Decide which sentences are confused or incorrect because of the way the **pronouns** have been used.
- Use **Worksheet 47** to re-write the sentences so that they are no longer confusing.

1 Dave and me will tell you about the planet Mars.

2 It would be impossible for a man to live on Mars because they need oxygen.

3 Mars and Pluto are two of the smallest planets who circle the Sun.

4 Patrick Moore is a famous British astronomer which is a person that studies the stars.

5 The Earth is the only one of the planets known to support life which makes them very special.

6 Rob spoiled Jason's talk on the planets and he was fed up.

Introduction as a group

Before you give your presentation, read the advice below.

- *Plan* who will say what and when, so that everyone has a part and everyone knows what they are doing.
- *Rehearse* your presentation. Try to be so familiar with your part that you can present your points without reading them.
- Introduce your presentation by giving it a *title of your own*, but remember the subject must be whether you think human beings could be living on Mars by 2098.
- Make points giving *both sides of the argument* – that people could be living on Mars, or couldn't be.
- Make use of *visual aids* in your talk – pictures, drawings, diagrams, posters, an OHT, flip chart, whiteboard etc.
- Look up and *speak clearly* – don't mumble.
- *Remember your audience* will be the rest of the class – make sure you speak to them in a way that they will understand and enjoy.
- Finish your talk by giving a definite *conclusion* about whether your group thinks that people will be living on Mars in 2098.

Use the planning frame on **Worksheet 48** to help you plan your presentation.

Development *on your own*

Listen carefully to each presentation and use **Worksheet 49** to assess and evaluate them.

Plenary

Decide which was the most successful presentation and why. Discuss how well each group worked together to produce their presentation.

A student giving a presentation

Reviewing what's been learnt

In this section you will have gained an understanding of the ways in which information and explanation texts are written. In particular:

- You have become better informed about the variety of sources that can be explored to provide you with a wealth of knowledge.
- You can find the answers to tricky questions with greater ease and speed, knowing where and how to look for information and explanations.
- You have developed your own writing skills and have engaged in a variety of writing tasks for different audiences and purposes.
- You have put your new-found skills to the test by working together to research information and explain your opinions to others.
- You know that it is important to acknowledge your sources.
- You have recognized the important role that descriptive writing plays by contributing interesting detail to a variety of texts.
- You have learnt about the influence of the ancient Greeks and Romans on our literary heritage.

Reflect on what you've learnt from this section and then, in your exercise book, write targets to improve your work. You should consider the following areas:

- Spelling
- Vocabulary
- Sentence structure
- Planning your writing
- Reading
- Speaking and listening.

My targets to improve my work are:
-
-
-
-
-
-

Persuade, argue, advise

Introduction

What comes to mind when you think of media texts, or when you think of poetry? Both are very different forms of writing but both have been shaped by the audience and purpose for which they have been written. In this section you will look closely at the features of a variety of media texts and poetry and understand how these features have been shaped by a particular purpose.

As you have already seen in earlier sections of this book, there are many different purposes to writing. This section will focus on just three of these: writing to persuade, argue or advise. Texts that persuade, argue and advise are all about trying to make people think or act in a certain way. When you advise, you often offer information and suggestions for how someone should behave in a particular situation. When you argue, you gather together all the reasons you can think of to support your viewpoint. When you persuade, you try to get people to agree with you and sometimes appeal more to their emotions than to their logic.

THE SUN SAYS
Bang to rights

WHAT on earth is happening at Winchester Prison?

Convict Kevin McGuigan – formerly chief medical officer at Parkhurst Jail – has been moved from his cell to a life of luxury in a £10,000-a-month clinic to the stars.

The people in charge of running HMP Winchester have decided, in their wisdom, that McGuigan should be serving his time at the Marchwood Priory where he is enjoying fine a la carte foods, a colour TV and video in his room and use of the swimming pool.

And guess who is paying for his stay at the exclusive retreat for the rich and the famous?

Key aims

In this section you will:

- Develop your understanding of, and skill in using, the devices that writers and speakers employ to make texts or speech persuade, argue or advise.
- Look at some of the ways that pre-1914 poetry creates particular effects, especially when arguing a case or persuading the audience.

Texts that persuade, argue, advi...

Aims

On these two pages you will:

- Identify key features of texts that aim to persuade, argue and advise.
- Learn key vocabulary relating to these texts.
- Explore how media texts are tailored to suit their audience and how writers use language to achieve particular effects.

Starter · as a class

1 Brainstorm all the types of media texts that you think:

- Persuade
- Argue
- Advise.

2 Now look at the words below. How many do you recognize? Use the grid on **Worksheet 50** to record your answers.

advertisement	factual
advice	identify
agreement	impartial
assumption	logical
audience	neutral/unbiased
balanced argument	opinion
biased argument	passive
broadsheet	purpose
brochure	repetition
complexity	rhetorical question
device	ridicule
editorial	tabloid
emotive	

Introduction · as a class

Read and discuss the four pieces of text on page 61. Your discussion should focus on a whole range of questions like the following:

- What is its purpose?
- Who is the audience?
- How would different audiences respond to each text?
- What type of text is it?
- What is its structure?
- What are the main language features?

The more you listen to everyone's contribution, the easier this sort of work becomes. Try to use the relevant words from the starter session in your discussion.

Development · as a group

Listen carefully while your teacher reads you the leaflet 'Here are five easy ways to make your environment a cleaner, greener place'. Then, in groups of four, see if you can fill in the grid on **Worksheet 51** relating to the purpose and audience of the text, what text type it is, its structure and how it's been written. Each member of your group should be ready to feed back on one of the headings.

Plenary

Listen to your classmates giving their opinions on this text and see if you agree with them. Add in your viewpoint. Remember to use the vocabulary from the starter session.

1

Kellogg's SPECIAL K red berries

As someone who enjoys *'Special K red berries'*, you are obviously aware of the benefits of **healthy eating**.

And, whilst folic acid is beneficial for everyone, it is especially important for women who are thinking of having a **baby**, who should increase their folic acid intake ...

2

A natural seaweed extract has been incorporated into each product in <u>The Body Shop</u> new <u>Skin Defensives</u>™ range to provide 7 new skin care products, designed to cleanse, protect and provide moisturisation. This unique ingredient provides an 'invisible shield', which when applied to skin helps to protect against daily environmental aggressors that we have come to expect in our fast-paced urban world: exhaust fumes, dirt, smog, grease and artificially high temperatures. The <u>Skin Defensives</u>™ range is suitable for all skin types and comprises an effective regime of skin solutions using exclusive formulations.

3

The transformation of Tottenham into a competent side, and of Anderton, Sheringham and Ruddock into England 'possibles', shows just how important confidence is.

Most Spurs fans could see that Anderton was classy but lacking in confidence and therefore gave him their support. It doesn't take a great deal of intelligence to draw on our experience of Chris Waddle and his progress from misfit to superstar. Yet some people proved they were incapable of learning and slagged off Anderton at Ipswich ... They've probably now deluded themselves into thinking that they always said Anderton was a great talent. It would be nice if they wrote to Darren, or to the programme or *Spur*, saying 'I apologize for being a sad case and realize I am incapable of forming any rational judgement about a player's ability.'

4

You will have heard of Center Parcs in the UK and you may even have enjoyed a stay in one, but did  you realize that there is a range of Center Parcs Villages on the continent as well? Choose from locations in Belgium, France, Germany and Holland.

Center Parcs is a unique combination of wonderful locations, state-of-the-art facilities and comfortable secluded accommodation.

The focus of each Village is a Subtropical Swimming Paradise, where spectacular water activities include wild water rapids, wave pools, toddlers' pools, flumes and whirlpool baths. Many more sports and leisure activities are on offer – from ten-pin bowling, canoeing to crazy golf – the list is endless.

Reading editorials

Aims

On these two pages you will:

- Identify different ways of expressing ideas and the devices used by writers and speakers to argue a case.
- Find out how these devices can be used to persuade people of your point of view.
- Identify key points in an argument.

Starter  as a group

Each group will be given slips of paper containing 24 different connectives that could be used in an argument (**Worksheet 52**). Sort them into the four categories below:

- *Ridicule* – anyone who thinks like this is an idiot.
- *Agreement* – all decent, sensible people think like this.
- *Neutrality* (unbiased) – there are different viewpoints, all of which need considering.
- *Complexity* – it's not easy to come to a definite view.

Introduction as a class

Thousands of different newspapers are published in Britain each week – national, regional and local papers; weekly and daily papers; **tabloids** and **broadsheets**. Newspapers consist of words, pictures and advertising. Their main purpose is to provide news and comment, but to keep their audience they must also entertain.

The extract on page 63 is a typical **editorial**, taken from *The Sun*, a tabloid newspaper. Before your teacher reads it to you, discuss which of the following you think it will be:

- Neutral/unbiased?
- Trying to stress the complexity of the issue?
- Written as if everyone must agree?
- Ridiculing anyone who contradicts its viewpoint?

as a group

1. Copy and fill in the chart below.
2. How does the structure of the article emphasize the points that it makes? Discuss the following:
- Length of the paragraphs and sentences
- Use of **rhetorical questions**
- Use of italics and underlining.
3. Find two facts and two opinions from the article.
4. You have probably never heard of Kevin McGuigan before reading this article. Do you think you now have a balanced picture of the situation?

Phrases used to make the reader dislike Kevin McGuigan and to put down and ridicule the people running the prison	Highly **emotive** words	Phrases aimed at encouraging the reader to agree with the editor

broadsheets larger format newspapers
editorial an article in a newspaper which gives the opinion of the editor
emotive designed to create emotion in the audience
rhetorical questions questions that don't require an answer; they are asked for dramatic effect
tabloids smaller format newspapers

THE SUN SAYS

Bang to rights

WHAT on earth is happening at Winchester Prison?

Convict Kevin McGuigan – formerly chief medical officer at Parkhurst jail – has been moved from his cell to a life of luxury in a £10,000-a-month clinic to the stars.

The people in charge of running HMP[1] Winchester have decided in their wisdom that McGuigan should be serving his time at the Marchwood Priory where he is enjoying fine a la carte[2] foods, a colour TV and video in his room and use of the swimming pool.

And guess who is paying for his stay at the exclusive retreat for the rich and the famous?

Britain's hard-pressed taxpayers.

This is a scandal of the highest order.

Even if wife-beating gun nut McGuigan is having psychiatric problems – why has he not been sent like every other prisoner to the secure unit normally used by the prison service?

And why is a man with an unhealthy obsession with firearms roaming free 200 yards from a primary school?

Sadly, the answer looks pretty clear.

Because his old mates running the prison have pulled some strings. We suspect the fact that he's a Master in his local Masonic Lodge[3] won't have hurt him either.

Home Secretary Jack Straw must sort this mess out immediately.

Kevin McGuigan is a nasty piece of work who should today be taken back to where he belongs – behind bars.

[1] *Her Majesty's Prison*
[2] *ordered as separate items from a menu – not a set meal*
[3] *branch of the Freemasons, a secret society*

Development

The article on **Worksheet 53** is taken from a broadsheet newspaper, *The Guardian*. This article is also trying to persuade its readers of its point of view. Read the article and then answer the questions below.

1 Look at the first paragraph. What two points does *The Guardian* make here?

2 The article contains two quotations. Which quotation supports *The Guardian*'s view? Why do you think the writer has included both of these quotations?

3 What is the difference between the format of *The Guardian* article and that of *The Sun* article?

4 Copy out and complete a table like the one below, listing all the techniques that the two newspapers have used to persuade their readers of their argument. Remember to use the correct terminology.

The Sun	The Guardian
Short punchy sentences	Quotations

Plenary

Discuss which article you think is more effective at arguing and persuading you of its point of view.

Writing editorials

Aims

On these two pages you will:

- Develop and express your own point of view clearly and effectively.
- Use a range of techniques to strengthen your case and persuade your audience.
- Investigate the passive, and discuss when you would use it.

Starter *as a group*

In your last term at primary school, you probably did some work on the **passive**. Both the editorials you looked at last lesson (pages 62–63) contained some sentences in the passive voice:

The Sun: 'Convict Kevin McGuigan … <u>has been moved</u> from his cell to a life of luxury'.

The Guardian: 'The British press <u>has been restrained</u> by an injunction'.

Today you will think about what difference the passive makes to how to interpret the meaning of a sentence.

1   In groups, sort the 15 sentences that you will be given (**Worksheet 54**) into three different categories (groups) so that each category has the same structure. (Look at the structure of the sentences, not their subject matter.)

2   Using your whiteboard or a piece of paper, add one extra example to each category.

3   Now try to analyse what each category has in common and what difference this structure makes to the meaning or emphasis of the sentences. See if you can give a heading to each category. Be prepared to discuss your findings.

4   When would you want to use the passive instead of the active?

Introduction *on your own*

Now it's your turn to be the editor. Select a headline from the two provided in the grid on page 65. Write a short editorial, which should *either* be in favour of boxing *or* condemn it. But before you start, your teacher will show you how you could develop your argument. Be prepared to suggest ways of making the argument persuasive. Include these features and techniques:

- Write as if you expect everyone to agree with you.
- Use a new paragraph for each new point you make.
- Link your paragraphs with connecting phrases (see the starter on page 62).
- Acknowledge the source of your information.

You could use one of the opening lines from the two provided in the grid on page 65 to help you, or you could make up the opening yourself. Select relevant information from the grid to back up your argument.

> **!** *Remember*, one way of writing as if you expect everyone to agree with you is to make readers think they are very sensible if they agree with the view you are putting, or should be locked up if they disagree with your view. You should do this at the beginning of the article, to set the tone straight away.

> **passive** the 'voice' used when the subject of a sentence is acted upon by the verb, for example, 'The man was arrested.' Compare this with 'The police arrested the man' (active).

Development *on your own*

Now try to make your editorial balanced. Using the heading 'Should boxing be banned or encouraged?', rewrite the beginning of your editorial to emphasize the strength of the arguments on both sides and to bring out the complexity of the issue. Use the relevant opening phrases from the starter activity on page 62, if you wish.

Plenary

Be prepared to read out sections of your editorials and explain the devices you've used to present a well-reasoned or biased argument. See if any of the sentences you have used in your editorial are in the passive, and consider what difference it makes.

homework

Redraft one of your editorials to make it as effective as possible.

Headlines

Every boy should box, Mr Blunkett
Make boxing part of the National Curriculum ◾◾◾

Ban this evil boxing now

Opening lines

What boys need to get back to the top of the class is boxing, a sport which channels all their natural laddish aggression.

How can a country claim to be civilized when it puts two young men in a ring and tells them to punch each other around the head in the name of sport?

Information

Boxing is only a dangerous sport if it is played by untrained people who do not follow the tight rules and is no more dangerous than many other sports like rugby or motor racing.
– Amateur Boxing Association

Training violent young people the skills of boxing teaches them self-control and discipline, as well as helping them realize that fighting should only take place in the ring.
– The Metropolitan Police Young Offenders Unit

Boxing can cause brain damage. Boxers experience memory loss, and concentration loss. Mohammed Ali, for example, has Parkinson's disease, which may have been caused by boxing.
– British Medical Association

Many boxers come from ethnic minorities. This promotes a stereotype of these groups as being violent.
– Campaign for Racial Equality

If boxing was banned then illegal fights would take place that could not be supervised by the authorities: there would be no rules and many people would suffer.
– Law Association

Boxing promotes the idea of violence as being acceptable. The fact that people can make vast amounts of money from fighting provides a role model that cannot be permitted.
– British Family Association

Advertisements

Aims

On these two pages you will:

- Investigate how adverts are composed to suit their audience.
- Explain, using the correct terminology, how adverts achieve a particular effect.
- Plan and write an advert.

Starter as a group

Advertisements take many forms, such as commercials on the television and radio, and classified and display adverts in the press. Advertising is a very important part of the media because without adverts much of the media could not afford to exist. Money paid by advertisers funds TV programmes, magazines, newspapers ... even CDs and websites.

Advertisements use many different devices to convey a particular message to their reader. A number of the devices they use have been listed below. You will be given cards with these devices, and cards with examples from advertisements (**Worksheet 55**). In groups, your task is to match each device to two examples – don't worry if some of the examples fit more than one device. Finally, see if you can work out why advertisers want to include such devices when writing adverts.

- The use of the second person
- Rhetorical questions
- Claim for effectiveness
- Clever word play
- Persuasive (weasel) words

- Association of ideas
- Rhymes and jingles
- Be exclusive, be extravagant
- Repetition
- Herd appeal

Introduction as a class

All adverts have been carefully designed to appeal to their target audience and persuade them to do or buy something. They use a range of devices to persuade us to do what they want, whether it be going on a wonderful holiday or buying a new computer. Look at the advert on page 67 and, as a class, consider the following questions:

- What do you think the purpose of the advert is?
- Who is its audience?
- What devices has it used to persuade its readers?
- What presentational devices has the advert used?
- Do you think it is effective?

Development as a group

Now it's your turn to plan and design two adverts. Your task is to market a new chocolate bar for two different audiences:

- Teenagers
- Adults.

You need to think carefully about what would appeal to your two different audiences so that you can plan and design your advert to suit their interests. Use **Worksheet 56** to brainstorm your ideas, then use your whiteboard or a piece of paper to draft ideas before producing your advert.

Plenary

Discuss the strengths and weaknesses of the adverts that you have produced.

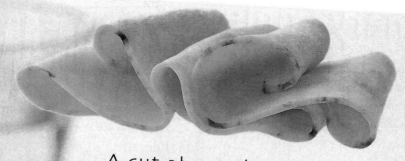

A cut above the rest
(by a healthy margin)

Who else but Bernard Matthews would come up with cooked turkey slices in the first place?

Who else would understand today's lifestyle demands healthy, low fat foods that still taste delicious?

Who else would insist upon only the best of cuts in a world where so much is quality-free?

Who else would provide such a varied range to help you ring the changes?

So, it's no surprise at all that Bernard Matthews is far and away the most popular name in cooked meats. Nothing else cuts the mustard.

Take my advice ...

Aims

On these two pages you will:

- Think about how texts that advise are structured, and what language features they use.
- Turn an information text into an advice text.
- Remind yourself of some common spelling patterns.

Starter `as a group`

In primary school you learnt how, in English, the same sounds can be spelt in a variety of different ways. In groups you will be given 35 words to sort into four rhyming groups plus one misfit (see **Worksheet 57**). Say all the words out loud and work out which word is the odd one out because its pronunciation doesn't fit any of the groups.

Now rearrange each group so that the words that are spelt similarly are next to each other. Work out how many different ways there are in each group for spelling the same sound and be prepared to feed your ideas back to the class.

Try to memorize these spelling patterns because you will be tested on some of these words.

Look at your spelling log. See if the patterns you have been working on will help you get any words right next time.

Introduction `as a class`

1 Discuss these questions:

- What kind of texts give advice? (If you get stuck, think of the sort of advice that may be given.)
- Where would you find such texts?
- Is there any difference between advice and persuasion? If so, what?

`in pairs`

2 Now get into pairs and look at the advice leaflet on page 69. Consider the following questions as you read the leaflet:

- What is the purpose of the leaflet?
- Who is the advice addressed to? What evidence is there to support your view?
- How are each of the sections structured?
- What is the connection between the first sentence of each section and the rest of that section?
- There are some very short sentences in the leaflet text. What effect do they have?
- What kind of language is used?
- How is the leaflet presented visually? Does this contribute to its purpose?

Use **Worksheet 58** to jot down your ideas, and be prepared to feed back your ideas to the class.

Development `on your own`

Now you are going to write an advice text of your own. But first your teacher is going to show you how. Look at the information about alcohol on **Worksheet 59**. Listen and watch carefully while your teacher turns the information in section A into advice in a teenage magazine about alcohol. Now it's your turn to transform the information in section B into advice for teenagers.

Remember to back up your advice with reasons and evidence. Try to use the language features that you identified in the leaflet 'The secret of making friends'.

Plenary

Feed back to the class what you have learnt about the structure and language features of advice texts.

The secret of making friends

Be patient and sensitive. No matter how much you like someone, don't demand too much, too soon; it may freak the other person out. No one likes to be pushed into things, nor to feel suffocated by another's attentions. Chill out, and let the relationship grow naturally.

Listen to your own conscience. If a <u>prospective</u>[1] friend does something that makes you feel uncomfortable, don't be afraid to break off. Likewise, if someone makes you feel bad about yourself, then dump them – they're no good for you. So that bad feelings aren't left to <u>ferment</u>[2] and therefore cloud whatever remains of the friendship, be up front and let them know what's bugging you.

Learn to be trusting. It's impossible to have a friendship if there is no element of trust. Both people have to be open, honest and not afraid to say no.

Be forgiving. Some people just can't cut it in the friendship stakes; they may let you down, stand you up, or blab something that was meant to be just between the two of you. What you've got to do is understand the limits of particular friendships.

You must not think that one disappointing friendship means that they'll all be disappointing. Learn to understand and forgive your friends their <u>shortcomings</u>.[3] There will be some people who will always be there for you, and there will be others who won't.

It's okay to have lots of friends. Without being at all disloyal, you can have different friends for different things. Some mates are ice-skating buddies, others are school pals and others you see only once a week at dance class. To some friends you will be an open book and they will know all your deepest, darkest fears. Other friends will only know the barest details. That's fine. Don't get worked up about making every friend a best friend.

[1] possible [2] build up, get worse [3] failings

homework

Complete a final draft of advice for teenagers about alcohol.

> **!** **Remember** to read your work carefully, improving it if necessary, and write a brief comment on how well you think you have completed the task.

Consolidation

Aims

In these two pages you will:

- Present and defend a point of view with supporting evidence.
- Listen to the opinions of others and evaluate their presentations.
- Use your knowledge of the roots of words to identify the meaning of new words.

Starter  as a group

Today you're going to look at just six words from the lists of key words that you've studied so far and see how many other words you know that are related to these words. The six words are:

> *imperative*   *identify*
> *emotive*   *instructions*
> *audience*   *logical*.

These words, plus 34 others, are on **Worksheet 60**.

1. First sort the words into six groups so that they all relate to one of the key words above.
2. If you can think of other words that could belong to these groups, note these down on your whiteboards or a piece of paper.
3. Now see if you can work out the meaning of all the other words and of the roots that link the words. Remember to use your knowledge about prefixes to help you.
4. Be prepared to share your ideas with the rest of the class.

Introduction   as a group

Now comes the real challenge. The class will be divided into eight groups. There are four passages on page 71 and two groups should analyse each of the extracts. Use the grid on **Worksheet 61a** to help you analyse your text. Use an OHT or blown-up copy of the extract to write your notes on (**Worksheet 61b**). You have about 15 minutes.

Development   as a group

The next task involves presenting your group's findings to the rest of the class. As two groups have studied each of the extracts, opinions may differ.

- Each pair of groups will be called on to take the role of the teacher and present their findings to the rest of the class, using the OHP.
- The speaking frame on **Worksheet 61a** will help you to plan your speech. Each member of the group should report back on an aspect of the text.
- Remember to speak the presentation, not read it.
- Only use the notes added to the OHT/blown-up version of the text.
- The rest of the class should use the listening frame on **Worksheet 62** to help compare the presentations of the two groups.

After the presentations, discuss as a class:

- The different points of view expressed by each group.
- The effectiveness of each presentation. How effective was each group at presenting their point of view? What methods did each group use in their presentation (e.g. emotive language)? What could they do to improve their presentation?

Plenary

In your groups, discuss how effective you think your group work was.

Did the class make any useful comments about your presentation?

How do you think you could improve (a) the way you worked together as a group, and (b) your presentation?

Share the results of your discussion with the class.

1

Useful tips on taking vitamins, minerals and supplements[1]

● Try to make sure your diet is as full of <u>nutrients</u>[2] as possible. This means eating a minimum of five portions of fruit and vegetables every day.

● Preferably eat them raw or steamed, to preserve the vitamin and mineral content. It's also important to buy fruit and vegetables regularly and store them in a cool, dark place.

● Vitamin C aids the <u>absorption</u>[3] of iron, so take your iron supplements with a glass of orange juice.

● Don't expect miracles overnight. The effects of supplements build up gradually and often you won't feel the benefits for several months.

[1] a pill that gives you more of something that's in your body
[2] a substance that provides nourishment
[3] taking something into the bloodstream

2

WIN! *a fantastic holiday in Tuscany*

Would you like to wake up in a luxury villa in the sun-drenched Tuscan countryside? Now you can … Tropicana Pure Premium, Britain's number one fruit juice, and Crystal Premier Italy, best-value specialist for travel to Italy, are offering two lucky Woman & Home readers the chance to each win a fabulous holiday, for up to four people, in the heart of Italy.

Tuscany offers peaceful countryside with glorious scenery, vineyards and hilltop hamlets, as well as the excitement of the great cities of Florence and Siena. Our fabulous holiday includes seven nights' accommodation in an apartment in a Crystal Premier villa, return flights and a car so you can explore the region.

3

The smack of good sense

Children and adults have this in common: they need rules to abide by, and like to know how far they can go. The trouble for parents has always been that they have so few disciplinary <u>sanctions</u>[1] with which to mark out the limits of <u>tolerable</u>[2] behaviour. We can send our children to their rooms – but what do we do when they refuse to go? We can threaten to stop their pocket money – but they know that they will be able to worm their way back into favour by the time pocket-money day comes round.

Used sparingly, and as a last resort, smacking can be an extremely effective way for parents to let their children know that they have overstepped the mark.

[1] punishments
[2] acceptable

4

3 speed vs the rest

The automatic choice of a 5 or 10 speed cycle may be a mistake – the humble 3 speed offers many advantages. Being less desired, it is less stolen; the gear mechanism is far more reliable and requires less maintenance. This sort of bike is usually sold with upright rather than racing handlebars; many people prefer the former in heavy traffic, as all controls are to hand … If you want a bike that will get you from A to B without problems the 3 speed is best.

Poetic technique

Aims

In these two pages you will:
- Look at some of the sound effects that poems use.
- Learn and revisit some of the key vocabulary and concepts relating to poetry.

Starter  as a group

In primary school you will have learnt about some of the sound effects used in poetry. In this starter you will revise some of the effects and the key terms relating to them.

Close your eyes and listen carefully while your teacher reads you a verse from a poem by Alfred Lord Tennyson.

Break, break, break,
On thy cold grey stones, O Sea!
And I would that my tongue could utter
The thoughts that arise in me.

> Alfred Lord Tennyson (1809–1892) was one of the most famous poets of the Victorian age. He was made Poet Laureate (the poet appointed as court poet of Britain) in 1850, a role he carried out for 42 years. His poetry reflects the concerns and issues of his age.

1 What mood do you think the poet was in when he wrote this?

2 Find an example of the following sound effects and say how they add to the mood of the verse:
- Alliteration
- **Assonance**
- Repetition.

3 Is the rhyming of the second and fourth lines effective?

4 There aren't any words in these lines that are perfect examples of onomatopoeia, like 'hiss' or 'quack'. But are there any words that you think the poet may have selected because the sound of the word helps reflect the mood he was trying to convey?

5 What is the rhythm of these lines? How has Tennyson achieved a rhythm where the words of the verse reflect the movement of the sea?

6 What connection do rhyme, repetition, assonance, alliteration and onomatopoeia have to rhythm?

> **assonance** the effect created by the repetition of vowel sounds

Introduction in pairs

Listen carefully as the poem on page 73, 'Song' by Christina Rossetti, is read to you. Then get into pairs and identify some of the poetic devices it uses. You should look for:
- Rhyme
- A clear, simple rhythm
- Alliteration
- Assonance
- Repetition
- Imagery.

Development on your own

1 • Who is the first **stanza** addressed to? What is the poet trying to say in these lines?
  • Who is the second stanza about? What attitude to death is expressed?

2 • In the first stanza what else might the grass above the grave been wet with?

• The word 'cypress' in the first stanza has two meanings. Cypress trees are conifers with dark foliage; they were often planted in graveyards. Cypress was also a type of cloth worn by people in mourning. Which meaning do you think Christina Rossetti had in mind? Or do you think she wanted her readers to think of both? Explain your answer.

• In the second stanza how does the poet describe what it is like to be dead?

• Does the poem suggest death is good or bad?

3 • The poem says 'sing no sad songs', but do you find the poem sad? Can you imagine the poem being sung in a cheerful voice? Give reasons for your answer.

• If you have time you could try fitting a tune to this song.

4 How successful do you think this song would be in persuading the poet's loved one not to mourn?

stanza verse; a group of lines with a particular pattern which is repeated throughout the poem

Plenary

What are your favourite lines from 'Song'? Explain your choice in a class discussion, using some of the technical language that you have revised in this lesson.

Christina Rossetti (1830–1894) was one of the greatest female poets of the 19th century. She first became known through her strange and sinister poem *Goblin Market*. In later life she suffered from ill health and devoted herself to her writing and to religious meditation. She took her religion so seriously that she refused to marry the man she loved because his religious beliefs differed from hers. Her poems are both intense and direct; many of them are melancholy in tone and focus on death. She was the sister of the Pre-Raphaelite poet and painter Dante Gabriel Rossetti.

Song

When I am dead, my dearest,
    Sing no sad songs for me;
Plant thou no roses at my head,
    Nor shady cypress tree:
Be the green grass above me
    With showers and dewdrops wet;
And if <u>thou wilt</u>,[1] remember,
    And if thou wilt, forget.

I shall not see the shadows,
    I shall not feel the rain;
I shall not hear the nightingale
    Sing on, as if in pain;
And dreaming through the twilight
    That doth not rise nor set,
<u>Haply</u>[2] I may remember,
    And haply may forget.

[1] you will
[2] perhaps

Death and the Victorians

Aims

In these two pages you will:
- Look at key features in the style, themes and values of Rossetti's poems.
- Understand how these features were influenced by the period in which she wrote.
- Experiment with the sound effects of language to make a piece of writing reflect your mood.

Starter *as a class*

Today you're going to start with an experiment in linking mood to the weather, just as Tennyson linked his sorrow and despair to the relentless movement of the sea in 'Break, Break, Break' (see page 72). In the old days many people around the world used to think, understandably, that thunder and lightning and storms meant the gods were angry. Think of a time when you've been very angry, or imagine someone who is very angry. Try to express this anger by using the sounds and imagery of a raging storm.

Use your whiteboards or a piece of paper to jot down some words, the sounds of which reflect your mood (for example, 'black'). Then link some of the words together, concentrating on creating appropriate sound effects through:
- Assonance
- Alliteration
- Repetition.

Play around with your ideas and see if you can come up with a few lines that you really like and which you could present to the class. As you write your

lines, think about the **stress** of the words and what sort of rhythm would be effective. You could use the verse from Tennyson's poem on page 72 as a model for your own writing.

stress the emphasis put on particular words, or on certain syllables or parts of words. For example, 'reflected' is stressed on the second syllable, 'flec'.

Introduction

The Victorians were much more comfortable about the idea of death than we are. For one thing they were much more familiar with it. Many babies died young and many mothers died in childbirth. Medicine was far less advanced at that time, so adults who became ill could do little but suffer and wait for nature to take its course. When old people were on the verge of death it was common for their families to gather around to be present for the person's last moments. Deathbed scenes were often described in literature and whether or not a person had a 'good' death was very important. Most Victorians believed firmly in God and saw death not as the end of life but as a new beginning. A good death was one in which the person concerned went willingly and calmly to meet his or her Maker; this was thought to indicate that the person had had a good and virtuous life.

Christina Rossetti was plagued by ill health for the latter part of her life. With no effective medicines and very little to relieve her pain she must often have felt that life was difficult and burdensome. For her, death was also a relief from pain and suffering.

Listen to the poem 'Remember' (right) as it is read out to you and be prepared to discuss these questions.

1 Who is speaking in the poem?

2 Who is being addressed?

3 How does Christina Rossetti describe the process of dying?

4 What does she want her lover to do when she is dead?

5 Does she expect her lover to remember her all the time?

6 Will she be upset if he doesn't?

7 Does she expect to remember her lover?

Discuss the following questions in groups, and be prepared to feed back your findings.

1 In what ways is 'Remember' similar in theme to 'Song' (page 73)?

2 Can you identify any similar poetic techniques?

3 'Remember' is a **sonnet**, whereas 'Song' is, obviously, a song. Look at the way the two poems rhyme and try to get an idea of their rhythms by reading them aloud.

4 Which poem do you find the more persuasive or comforting for Christina Rossetti's lover?

5 How do the two poems reflect the ideas and concerns of the age in which they were written? (Think about the information in the introduction.) Use evidence from the poems to support your opinion.

sonnet a poem with 14 lines and a fixed rhyme scheme

Remember

Remember me when I am gone away,
Gone far away into the silent land;
When you can no more hold me by the hand,
Nor I half turn to go yet turning stay.
Remember me when no more day by day
You tell me of our future that you planned:
Only remember me; you understand
It will be late to counsel then or pray.
Yet if you should forget me for a while
And afterwards remember, do not grieve:
For if the darkness and <u>corruption</u>[1] leave
A <u>vestige</u>[2] of the thoughts that once I had,
Better by far you should forget and smile
Than that you should remember and be sad.

[1] *decay (especially of a corpse)*
[2] *trace*

Development on your own

You will find 'Up-hill', another poem by Christina Rossetti, on **Worksheet 63**. Listen and follow carefully while the poem is being read to you, then answer the questions on the worksheet.

Plenary

Discuss what you think the three poems by Rossetti that you have studied have in common. You should think about the ideas they contain and the techniques they use.

Analysing poetry

Aims

In these two pages you will:

- Look at the techniques of persuasion in two poems.
- Write a persuasive argument yourself.
- Investigate terms of comparison.

Starter  in pairs

Look at the sentences on **Worksheet 64** and see if you can come up with some rules about how you compare things.

Introduction in pairs

Listen carefully while your teacher reads two poems (written in the form of **epitaphs**) from *Spoon River Anthology* (see page 77). The first tells you Mrs Charles Bliss's view of her marriage; the second reveals Reverend Wiley's view.

1 Look at the questions on the first poem at the bottom of **Worksheet 65** and discuss them with a partner.

2 Now consider Reverend Wiley's view about the Bliss family in the second poem by discussing the following questions. Be prepared to feed back your ideas.

- What kind of character was Reverend Wiley? Point to evidence in the poem to support your view.
- If Reverend Wiley was a preacher, he should have been able to put his case persuasively. How does he attempt to do this in the poem?
- Are you persuaded? If not, why not?
- After you have read the poem, do you feel more or less sympathy for Mrs Bliss? Do you think the poet intended you to feel this?

Development on your own

Imagine that you are one of the Bliss children. Write a first draft for a tombstone epitaph giving the child's view of being brought up in a divided home. Here are some suggestions:

- Focus on the power of your argument and the images that you use. See how effective Edgar Lee Masters's style is, and use this if you can.
- You would be full of bottled up anger and resentment. Your mother, Mrs Bliss, has used a gardening image to express her bitterness. You might want to use some of your 'sound' words that you worked on last lesson (page 74) and use storm imagery.
- The language of Reverend Wiley's epitaph is quite **abstract**. You might want to make your epitaph more persuasive by using **concrete** imagery. You may like to use the imagery of plants, as Mrs Bliss did in her epitaph.

abstract based on thoughts and ideas rather than physical objects
concrete based on physical objects rather than abstract ideas
epitaph the words inscribed on a tombstone

Plenary

Listen to the opening lines of some of the epitaphs you have drafted. In pairs, read each other's draft so far and make suggestions as to how each draft could be improved.

homework

Redraft your epitaph, and inscribe the final version on the tombstone on **Worksheet 66**.

! **Remember** to read your work carefully, improve it if necessary and write a brief comment on how well you think you have completed the task.

1

Mrs Charles Bliss

Reverend[1] Wiley advised me not to divorce him
For the sake of the children,
And Judge Somers advised him the same.
So we stuck to the end of the path.
But two of the children thought he was right,
And two of the children thought I was right.
And the two who sided with him blamed me,
And the two who sided with me blamed him,
And they grieved for the one they sided with.
And all were torn with the guilt of judging,
And tortured in soul because they could
    not admire
Equally him and me.
Now every gardener knows that plants grown
    in cellars
Or under stones are twisted and yellow
    and weak.
And no mother would let her baby suck
Diseased milk from the breast.
Yet preachers and judges advise the raising of
    souls
Where there is no sunlight, but only twilight,
No warmth, but only dampness and cold–
Preachers and judges!

[1] the title given to a church minister

2

Rev. Lemuel Wiley

I preached four thousand sermons,
I conducted forty revivals,[1]
And baptized many converts.[2]
Yet no deed of mine
Shines brighter in the memory of
    the world,
And none is treasured more by me:
Look how I saved the Blisses
    from divorce,
And kept the children free from
    that disgrace,
To grow up into moral men
    and women,
Happy themselves, and a credit to
    the village.

[1] meetings to encourage religious life
[2] admitted non-believers into the church in a formal ceremony

Edgar Lee Masters (1868–1950) spent his childhood in the state of Illinois, America. He decided to paint a picture of small-town life in words by giving voices to the dead of an imaginary town, Spoon River. *Spoon River Anthology* is a collection of 244 poetic epitaphs which together provide a picture of the narrow opinions, bitterness and hypocrisy of small-town life.

Poetry that persuades

Aims

In these two pages you will:

- Investigate the forms in which poetry is written.
- Understand how particular poetic effects are achieved, using the correct language to describe them.
- Express a view clearly, using evidence to support your opinion.

Starter  as a group

Poems come in many different forms. Look at the list below and then, in groups, try to identify the forms of the five poems on **Worksheet 67**.

1 **Elegy**. A sad poem or song about someone who has died.
2 **Haiku**. A Japanese form of poetry. Haikus usually have three lines.
3 **Limerick**. A five-line comic verse with the rhyming scheme a a b b a.
4 **Lyric poem**. A poem that focuses on an important moment in the poet's life, and is concerned with the emotions evoked by that event.
5 **Narrative poem**. A poem that tells a story. Earlier narrative poems, called ballads, have short, regular verses with a rhyme scheme.
6 **Rap poem**. A form of oral poetry, associated with Caribbean and Afro-Caribbean cultures, which has a strong rhythm and rapid pace.
7 **Shape poem**. A poem in which the layout of the words reflects the subject, or an aspect of the subject. Also called concrete poem.
8 **Sonnet**. A poem of 14 lines, often in two stanzas of eight lines then six lines. Sonnets follow a variety of rhyme schemes.

Introduction as a class

You met William Shakespeare in an earlier lesson (see page 44). Although Shakespeare was primarily a dramatist, his plays contain much poetry. The poetry is generally **blank verse**, but rhymed verse is also sometimes used for special effect.

Shakespeare's audience would have enjoyed hearing a well-constructed and well-argued speech. It was something they had been taught to appreciate. The art of making speeches to persuade an audience was an important part of a boy's education at school and university (girls didn't go to school), where it was called rhetoric.

All sorts of different techniques are used in a persuasive speech, such as:

- Similes, metaphors and personification to create powerful imagery
- The use of alliteration, assonance and repetition
- Drawing the listener in by appealing to them directly
- Changes in tone and direction for variety and interest
- Emotive language to move the audience
- Painting pictures that tug at the heart-strings.

Imagine that you are about to go out and fight a battle. Listen carefully while your teacher introduces and reads to you Henry V's speech to his soldiers before the Battle of Agincourt (page 79). Think about how Shakespeare has made this speech very persuasive.

blank verse verse that doesn't rhyme. It often has a regular pattern of ten syllables with five stresses in each line.

Development *as a group*

1 In groups of five, study King Henry's speech (below). Each person in the group should choose one of the five sections of the speech and decide what techniques Henry is using to persuade his men to join him willingly in the fight. Use the grid on **Worksheet 68** to record your ideas.

2 Then get together as a group and decide how persuasive you think this speech is. Be prepared to feed back your opinions.

> **!** **Remember** to pay particular attention to the use of the third person ('he') and the first person plural ('we').

Plenary *as a class*

Elect a spokesperson for each group, who should feed back the group's ideas to the class.

homework

Next lesson you will pretend that you are the manager of a group of sportspeople just before a major sporting event. You will be asked to draft a speech to spur your team on to victory. In preparation for this activity, note down some key points you think you'd want to make in your speech.

The speech below, which is in blank verse, comes from Shakespeare's play Henry V. *It is the morning of 25 October 1415, St Crispin's day, and Henry's small, bedraggled army is facing a hugely superior French force at Agincourt in northern France. The king addresses his troops before the battle.*

[1] … he which hath no stomach to this fight,
Let him depart; his passport shall be made,
And <u>crowns for convoy</u>[1] put into his purse:
We would not die in that man's company
That <u>fears his fellowship to die with us</u>.[2]

[2] This day is called the feast of Crispian.
He that outlives this day, and comes safe home,
Will stand a tip-toe when this day is nam'd,
And rouse him at the name of Crispian.
He that shall live this day, and see old age,
Will yearly on <u>the vigil</u>[3] feast his neighbours,
And say, 'Tomorrow is Saint Crispian'.
Then will he strip his sleeve and show his scars,
And say, 'These wounds I had on Crispian's day.'

[3] Old men forget: yet all shall be forgot,
But he'll remember, with <u>advantages</u>,[4]
What feats he did that day. Then shall our names,
Familiar in his mouth as household words—
Harry the King, <u>Bedford and Exeter,
Warwick and Talbot, Salisbury and Gloucester</u>[5]—
Be in their flowing cups freshly remember'd.

[4] This story shall the good man teach his son;
And <u>Crispin Crispian</u>[6] shall ne'er go by,
From this day to the ending of the world,
But we in it shall be remembered—
We few, we happy few, we band of brothers;
For he to-day that sheds his blood with me
Shall be my brother; be he ne'er so vile,
This day <u>shall gentle his condition</u>;[7]

[5] And gentlemen in England now a-bed
Shall think themselves accurs'd they were not here,
And <u>hold their manhoods cheap</u>[8] whiles any speaks
That fought with us upon Saint Crispin's day.

From Shakespeare, *Henry V*, Act 4 scene 3

[1] money for travel
[2] fears keeping us company might lead to his death
[3] the night before the feast day
[4] a little exaggeration
[5] titles of leading noblemen
[6] Crispin and Crispian were two brothers
[7] shall be raised to the rank of gentleman
[8] feel ashamed of their manhood

William Shakespeare (1564–1616) is perhaps the most famous playwright of all time. He was born and died at Stratford-upon-Avon in Warwickshire, but spent most of his life acting and writing plays in London. He also wrote many sonnets.

Consolidation

Aims

In these two pages you will:

- Review the main methods used by presenters to explain, persuade or argue a case.
- Present a point of view, giving your evidence.
- Compare different points of view that have been expressed.
- Investigate terms of qualification.

Starter *on your own*

Look at the following five sentences:

1 It's <u>mainly</u> right.
2 It's <u>slightly</u> wrong.
3 He's a <u>fully</u> paid up member of the club.
4 It's <u>completely</u> dark by five.
5 The water's <u>fairly</u> hot.

The **adverbs** in each sentence have been underlined. These words 'qualify', or alter the meaning of, each sentence by adding information. See if you can replace each of the underlined words with another word or phrase so that the meaning of the sentence stays the same.

Be prepared to explain your ideas to the rest of the class.

> **adverb** a word or phrase that tells you more about a verb, an adjective or even a whole sentence

Introduction *in pairs*

1 In pairs, brainstorm all the techniques of persuading, arguing and advising that you can remember from this section. Use the spider diagram on **Worksheet 69** to record your ideas.

2 Get together with another pair and share your ideas. Add more legs to your spider if the other pair come up with good techniques that you missed.

Development *in pairs*

1 Pretend that you are the manager of any group of sportspeople just before a major sporting event. In pairs, draft the speech that is going to spur them on to victory. You need to present all your points in as persuasive a way as you can.

- Use the techniques that you recorded in your spider diagram.
- Look back at the devices Shakespeare employed (page 79).
- Remember to grab your listeners' attention at the beginning of the speech, and to end on a high note, too.

2 Take it in turns to deliver the speech and decide how it could be amended to make it more powerful and persuasive.

3 Redraft your speech.

4 Practise delivering it effectively.

Plenary

Some of you will deliver your speeches to the class. The rest of the class should use **Worksheet 70** to record how persuasive they think the speeches are. Share your views in a whole class discussion.

Reviewing what's been learnt

In this section you have developed your understanding, and skill in using, the devices that writers and speakers employ to make their texts or speeches persuade, argue or advise. In particular, you have:

- Identified the key features of texts that aim to persuade, argue and advise
- Understood how their structure, language features and key devices are tailored to suit their purpose and audience
- Used these features when writing your own editorial, advert and advice leaflet
- Presented and defended a point of view with supporting evidence.

Also in this section you have looked at some of the techniques that have been used in poetry to create a particular effect and how these techniques can be used to express meaning. You have applied this knowledge in your own writing. You have also developed an understanding of how the period in which a poet wrote can often be reflected in the features, themes and values of their poems.

Reflect on what you've learnt from this section and then, in your exercise book, write targets to improve your work. You should consider the following areas:

- Spelling
- Vocabulary
- Sentence structure
- Planning your writing
- Reading
- Speaking and listening.

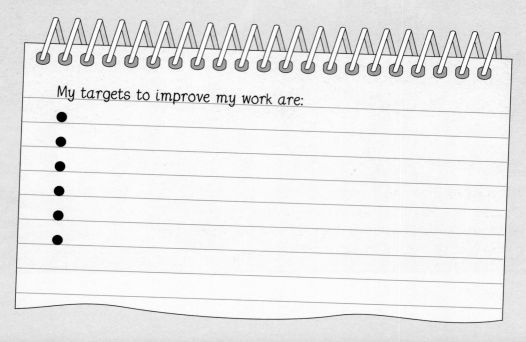

My targets to improve my work are:
-
-
-
-
-
-

Analyse, review, comment

Introduction

When you analyse something, such as a story, drama or review, you look at it in detail to help you understand it better. This can involve working out what the main features are and how they all fit together.

When you comment on something, you express a view based on your analysis of it. It is often useful to make notes when you analyse something as this will help you to develop your ideas and structure your comments.

When you review something such as a book or film, you write an account expressing your opinion. 'Review' also means to look again at something, like a piece of work, and reflect on its effectiveness and comment on how it could be improved.

In this section you will be analysing the main ingredients of drama so that you can evaluate, comment on and review script extracts and performances. You will also consider how to analyse and review your work in other subject areas.

Key aim

In this section, you will:
- Develop your skills in analysing, reviewing and commenting on drama, as well as working in a group to write and perform a script.

Playscripts

Aims

In these two pages you will:

- Compare a cartoon, a story and a play version of the same story.
- Look more closely at how playscripts differ from other genres of writing.
- Use speech punctuation accurately in a variety of sentences.

Starter *in pairs*

1 Look at the cartoon on **Worksheet 71**. You will notice that it has pictures and no words.
2 Discuss what the cartoonist is trying to communicate.
3 Now think of the story that these pictures could be illustrating. Share your ideas with the class.

Introduction *as a group*

In this lesson you will begin to look at the way drama is different from other forms or 'genres' of writing. In order to do this, you will start by comparing the written form and structure of three different genres: a cartoon, a play and a story.

Look carefully at the three versions of the same story (page 85) and then answer the following questions for each of the extracts in turn:

1 How do you know what the setting of the story is?
2 How do you know who is speaking?
3 How do you know what words are actually spoken?

4 How do you know what sort of mood Andy is in?
5 If Florrie had been thinking something but didn't say it, how would it have been shown?
6 What do you notice about the structure and layout?

Use **Worksheet 72** to write down your ideas. Be prepared to feed back your findings.

Development *on your own*

1 Look again at the wordless cartoon on **Worksheet 71** and turn it into a cartoon with words. Remember to use the proper cartoon conventions. Look at the Andy Capp cartoon to remind yourself about how to lay out a cartoon.

> **!** Make each character speak only once per picture, keep the speech short and make the big person speak first. Write in the words before drawing the speech or thought bubble round them.

2 Now turn your cartoon into a play. Remember to use a script format to establish where the scene is set (scene setting) and any hints to the actors about how to say their lines (stage directions). Look at the play version of the Andy Capp cartoon to help you.

Plenary

Each person should think of one difference between the playscript and story genre and then feed back to the rest of the class.

homework

Write your cartoon story as a story with direct and indirect speech (see pages 26–29).

 Remember to read your story through carefully, correcting any mistakes. Write a comment at the bottom telling your teacher how well you think you have done this piece of work.

When your work is returned, add any words that you misspelt to your spelling log.

1 *A day in the life of Andy Capp (cartoon form)*

2

A day in the life of Andy Capp (play form)

Setting → *(The scene is set in Andy Capp's sitting room. As always he is sitting on the sofa.)*

Stage directions →

FLORRIE *(carrying some dishes past the sofa)* You look miserable sitting there, Andy. Why don't you have a game of snooker?

ANDY Florrie, would you play with a bloke who fiddles the score and moves the balls when you're not looking?

FLORRIE I would not!

ANDY *(miserably)* Neither will Chalkie!

3 *A day in the life of Andy Capp (story form)*

Andy Capp was sitting miserably in the corner of the couch staring into space. His poor wife, Florrie, was busy clearing away the dishes as usual. As she walked past her husband, she turned to him and said: 'You look miserable sitting there, Andy. Why don't you have a game of snooker?'

Andy looked up and shouted after her, 'Florrie, would you play with a bloke who fiddles the score and moves the balls when you're not looking?'

'I would not!' replied Florrie indignantly.

'Neither will Chalkie!' retorted Andy, once again staring blankly from under the peak of his cap.

From novel to playscript (1)

Aims

In these four pages you will:

- Look more closely at dramatic techniques and understand the importance of audience.
- Investigate how a written story can be turned into a playscript, and analyse what difference this makes to the material.
- See if you can become an expert on the apostrophe.

Starter  as a group

You will have learnt in primary school about apostrophes for omission and possession. You're going to go over this now. Aim to become an expert on this so you can explain clearly when, why and where apostrophes are needed, and then you can help anyone who has problems with this.

1 You will be given a number of correctly punctuated sentences (**Worksheet 73**). Sort them into the three categories below:

A. Sentences that include apostrophes of possession

B. Sentences that include apostrophes of omission

C. Sentences that don't need any apostrophes.

2 Analyse group A. This is the group that causes the most problems. Some of the words end with 's (apostrophe + s) and some end s' (s + apostrophe). Divide the sentences into these two groups and see if you can come up with a simple explanation for why this is.

3 Analyse group B. Work out a simple explanation for why some of the words include apostrophes.

4 Finally look at group C. Discuss why some people might be confused by these sentences and want to put apostrophes in some of the words. Can you come up with some simple rules to help people out here?

Introduction as a class

Dramas are very different from stories, as you began to discover from your work on cartoons (pages 84–85). The most important difference is that dramas are written to be performed to an audience, rather than read from the page. Audiences watch dramas to be entertained. So when playwrights develop a script for a play, they need to make sure that they hold the audience's attention and interest.

Here are some of the challenges that a playwright faces.

Time factor

Stories can cover whole lifetimes. But who's going to sit around for a lifetime watching a drama? Dramas usually only last up to two or three hours, so playwrights have to condense a lot of events into a small space of time.

How to convey description

In stories, a lot of information about characters, setting and situations is conveyed through detailed descriptions. As the audience will be watching a drama rather than reading the script, the playwright needs to convey these descriptions in other ways. How do you think a playwright might do this?

Holding the audience's attention

A drama needs to hold the audience's attention throughout and make them think about what is happening. Playwrights do this by making the playscripts 'dramatic' or exciting by using a number of different *dramatic techniques*. These can include:

- Adding moments of tension or excitement – such as moments when the audience isn't sure what's going to happen
- Creating a change of mood or atmosphere between scenes: an action-packed scene might be followed by a slower-paced scene
- Using a subplot to act as a contrast to the main plot
- Using a narrator to give an insight to the characters' feelings and to create a greater intimacy with the audience.

in pairs

The extract on page 88 is taken from an autobiography, *Twopence to Cross the Mersey*, by Helen Forrester. Listen as your teacher reads you the extract and think about how you would convert it into a playscript. In particular, think about how you would convey the atmosphere and how you would express Helen's thoughts.

Development as a group

Helen Forrester gave her permission to have the story turned into a play, which was then written by Valerie Windsor. In groups, read the playscript on page 89. When you have read it, compare it with the story extract, answering the following questions:

1 What do you notice about the amount of dialogue in both versions?
2 What parts of the story have been cut?
3 How is the atmosphere and setting conveyed in the playscript?
4 What are Helen's feelings for Edward in paragraph 2 of the story? How is this conveyed in the playscript?
5 How is Helen feeling in paragraph 5 of the story? How is this conveyed in the playscript?
6 In the playscript, why does Helen attempt to jump after the sailor has called out to her?
7 Why does Helen speak directly to the audience at the end of the scene?
8 Do you think the changes that have been made to the story make the playscript more 'dramatic'? Give reasons for your opinion.

Plenary

Share your findings with the class. Listen carefully and see if other groups come up with good points you hadn't thought of.

What do you think is the main difference between reading a book and seeing the same story as a play or a film?

From novel to playscript (2)

Storyline: At this point in her story fourteen-year-old Helen is so desperate that she wants to throw herself into the River Mersey to end her life. She lives in great poverty and is treated very badly by her parents. She has to spend all her time looking after her baby brother, Edward, because her mother can't be bothered.

A foggy September day saw Edward being pushed in the Chariot along the gently heaving Georges Landing-Stage. The Birkenhead ferry was slowly leaving the stage and vanishing into the misty river. The shore hands were coiling up their ropes ready for the next ferry-boat. Upon the invisible river invisible ferries clanged their bells and were answered by freighters sounding their foghorns. Behind me, the lights of the Royal Liver and Cunard buildings barely <u>penetrated</u>[1] the <u>unseasonable</u>[2] gloom. At one end of the landing-stage a pilot-boat had just returned from beyond the bar, after collecting the pilot from an outgoing ship. At the other end a group of customs officers chatted, their raincoats gleaming with moisture. No passengers were waiting for the ferries.

Carefully, I tucked the cover round the sleeping Edward and made sure that the hood protected him from the slight wind which occasionally lifted the fog. I hoped someone kind would find him and take him home and love him. I propped the pram against a post so that it could not roll into the water, and left it.

Very slowly, I approached the chain fence that stopped pedestrians from falling off the edge of the landing-stage. When I felt its cold links against my shins, I paused. Some three feet still separated me from the swirling water, invisible for the moment because of the mist.

I stepped over the fence and took a couple of paces more. I could see the water now. Everyone in Liverpool knew that if anybody fell into the water at the end of the landing-stage the tremendous <u>undertow</u>[3] would suck them right under the stage to certain death. It would not take long.

I was shivering violently, <u>nauseated</u>[4] by the thought of the oily water and the choking death which seemed to be the only available way of committing suicide. At the same time I could not bear the thought of turning back into a life which was <u>unendurable</u>[5] to me.

I took a large breath preparatory to jumping.

A huge paw clamped suddenly down on my shoulders and a voice behind me said, 'And phwhat in the Name o' God do you think you're doing?'

The sudden interruption was so terrifying that my knees buckled under me, and another huge hand grasped the back of my dress, and I was yanked bodily back over the fence.

Supported only by the iron grip on my shoulder, I found myself looking at the middle fastenings of a sailor's waterproofs. I followed the line of the fastenings upwards with my eyes and found myself looking into the <u>rubicund</u>[6] face of the pilot who had just landed. The water dripping off the peak of his cap did not <u>obscure</u>[7] the concern in his eyes.

I could not answer. I was fainting.

'Mother of Heaven, you gave me a fright,' he said sharply.

I must have fainted completely, because the next thing I remember was being in a little canteen and having hot tea forced between my lips by a careworn woman in grubby white.

[1] *broke through*
[2] *unexpected for the season*
[3] *current under the surface of the water*
[4] *sickened*
[5] *unbearable*
[6] *ruddy, reddish*
[7] *hide*

Slowly, **Helen** *pushes the pram up the slope to the Pier Head and angles the pram so that* **Edward** *is looking out over the water.*

Helen (*to Edward*) I'm going to leave you here, Edward. You'll be all right. Sit up, look. There's a good boy. There's the Birkenhead Ferry. See. You watch the boats. Somebody will find you. I've written your address inside the hood. You just watch the boats.

Helen *then goes over to the edge of the Pier Head. The pram should be angled so that* **Edward** *couldn't possibly see her. She leans for a moment on the railings. We hear the sounds of the river: gulls, boats etc. An old* **sailor** *is strolling up the slope.* **Helen** *looks round, and, failing to see the sailor, makes up her mind and slips under the railings. She balances* <u>precariously</u>[1] *on the very edge of the Pier Head. Then she closes her eyes. After a moment we hear her softly counting.*

Helen One … two … three …

But the **sailor** *has spotted her.*

Sailor Here, hang on! What in the name of God …!

Helen bends her knees to spring. The **sailor** *grabs at her cardigan and pulls her back from the edge.*

Sailor Mother in heaven, you gave us a fright. Hey, come on … come on … don't pass out on me … Here, have a swig of this … warm you up.

Helen *is shaking and crying. The* **sailor** *holds her and pulls a small bottle of rum from his pocket and forces her to drink. It makes her splutter.*

Sailor Jesus, girl, you can't be that desperate to get out of Liverpool, can you? And even if you are … here, have another (*And he offers her another swig …*) Even if you are, I promise you there's better ways out than trying to swim across the Mersey. (*He has taken off his coat and wraps it round her shoulders.*) You sit there a minute. I'll see if I can find you a cup of tea. There's a canteen across the road.

Helen (*narrating*) He was quite right. There *were* better ways out of Liverpool. What a stupid thing to do. And I had *still* been expecting all the time that someone would wave a magic wand and change everything. No, if I wanted change, then I began to realise that I'd have to make it happen myself.

[1] *dangerously*

Aims

In these two pages you will:

- Analyse how a TV producer uses sound, image and text in the title sequence of a programme to produce particular effects.
- Analyse an episode of a television soap opera to establish the plot pattern and structure.
- Test out your analysis to see if the pattern is repeated by other soaps.
- Revise the use of the apostrophe.

Starter *on your own*

How well have you remembered about when to use apostrophes? Listen carefully to each sentence your teacher reads you and write down on your whiteboard or a piece of paper any word that needs an apostrophe. The sentences are from the play extract you looked at on page 89 and from another play you're going to be looking at on pages 94–95.

Introduction *as a class*

A key part of any successful drama is the plot. As with stories, dramatic plots generally follow a similar format and contain:

- A gripping introduction
- A developing plot
- A complication
- A crisis
- A resolution.

As a class, discuss a film you have watched recently and decide whether it followed this format.

One development in drama in the last forty years has been the rise of the soap opera. Traditionally plays tell one major story with perhaps a subplot or two running alongside the main plot, which contrasts with, or throws light on, the main action. Soap operas, on the other hand, have a number of completely different plots and the focus jumps rapidly from one plot to another. The plots are linked by location: they focus on looking closely at the lives of people living or working in a particular place.

You are going to watch the first few minutes from a typical soap opera plus the ending of a half-hour episode.

1   First of all, however, you're going to analyse what the title sequence of the programme tells you. Your teacher is going to give you a grid like the one below to help you do this (**Worksheet 74**). While watching the title sequence of a soap opera note down what music you hear and what images and text you see. Discuss with a partner what effect you think this creates and be prepared to discuss your ideas with the rest of the class so that you can decide why the producer chose to begin the programme in this way.

Feature	Notes	Effect
Music/sound		
Images		
Moving images		
Still images		
Text		

2 Now it's time to watch a few minutes of the programme.

Your teacher is going to provide you with a note-taking analysis grid (**Worksheet 75**) to help you work out the following:

- How many story lines are there running in this extract?
- How much time is spent on each story and how often is it revisited during the extract?
- Does the programme end with a cliffhanger?

You may also want to consider:

- Which stories are just developing and which ones are rising to a crisis.

- Is there a lead story or are they all equal?
- Are there any signs of a new plotline just bubbling to the surface? You could work out symbols to represent these, such as * = new plotline.

You are not going to have much time to write down the information on your grid. Work out what abbreviations you could use. Your teacher will provide you with the names of the key characters and locations you will be seeing, so you could just use the initials of their names.

Below is an example of how to fill the grid in. It's an analysis of the first two minutes of *Brookside* when the neighbours are finally aware that Susannah Morrissey is dead.

Minute	Storyline 1	Storyline 2	Storyline 3
1	SM's home – dead. Ex-hubs Max & Di. Di goes to her house to phone police	Cut to Mick's house – kissing new 'girlfriend'*	
2	Cut to Di's household – phoning police		Cut to Rachel's – worrying about husband – out late

Key to abbreviations
SM – Susannah Morrissey
Di – Di Murray
* – new plotline

Development (on your own)

Watch the recording and fill in your grid as accurately as you can. You will probably need to watch the recording twice.

Plenary

Discuss your findings as a class. What pattern, if any, seems to have emerged?

homework

Now test out your findings on a different soap opera by analysing the first few minutes of any soap opera currently on television. See if it follows the same formula as the one you watched in school and briefly write up your findings. You could begin your summary like this.

I have analysed the structure of the opening instalments of two different soap operas. I have discovered that ...

Aims

In these four pages you will:

- Understand how characters are portrayed in dramas.
- See how the English language is full of words taken from other languages.

Starter  in pairs

You're going to start today with a bit of close analysis of the origins of the language that we speak.

The English language contains more words than any other language in the world. This is partly because English has incorporated words from such a wide range of other languages. Latin, the language of the Romans who occupied Britain between AD 43 and 410, provides the roots for many thousands of English words and place names.

Below is a short extract from the Requiem (a church service for the dead), followed by a translation. In the Roman Catholic church the Requiem was said in Latin until the 20th century, and the Latin words are still used in musical settings of the service.

> Mors stupebit et natura
> Cum resurget creatura,
> Judicanti responsura.
> Liber scriptus proferetur
> In quo totum continetur
> Unde mundus judicetur.

> Death and nature shall be stunned,
> When mankind arises,[1]
> To render[2] account before the judge.
> The written book[3] shall be brought,
> In which all is contained,
> Whereby the world shall be judged.

[1] *at the Last Judgement, when the dead are raised*
[2] *give*
[3] *the book of judgement*

Complete the grid on **Worksheet 76** by giving the translation for each Latin word and adding any other English words that you think might be related to this Latin word. If you're wondering why there are far more words in the English lines than in the Latin ones, Latin adds suffixes onto words to indicate such things as person, tense and movement towards.

Introduction as a class

In drama it is important that the playwright creates characters that the audience is interested in and can have feelings for, whether they are feelings of like or dislike. If the audience isn't interested in the lead characters, it won't care what happens to them.

The extract on pages 94–95 is taken from a play called *Stand Up, Nigel Barton* by Dennis Potter. Since it is set in a classroom, you've got the perfect setting for reading out the extract as a class. (Note, though, that the play is set in the 1950s and the classroom would have been very formal, with rows of separate desks.)

Read the playscript as a class. Two people should volunteer to be Nigel Barton and Georgie Pringle. Your teacher will be Miss Tillings and the rest of the class can be her class in the playscript. As you're reading, think about the characters and how and what we learn about them.

When you've read the extracts discuss your impressions of:

- Miss Tillings
- Nigel Barton
- Georgie Pringle.

This extract reveals a lot about Nigel's character in a number of ways:

1 The way he behaves, as outlined in the stage directions

- Look at the stage directions in lines 1–9. What do they tell us about Nigel?

2 What he says and how he says it (the dialogue)

- Which line lets the audience know that Nigel's school memories are very painful to him? How has the playwright achieved this effect?
- What does the word 'proudly' in line 13 tell us about Nigel?

3 Other people's behaviour towards him

- What impression of Nigel do we get from Miss Tillings's behaviour and comments to him?

What makes these scenes dramatic? Consider the following parts of the playscript:

- Compare what Miss Tillings says to Nigel and what she says to the rest of the class. What effect does this have?
- What is the effect of the lines that Nigel recites in lines 24–25 and 38–39?
- When Georgie Pringle volunteers to read from the Bible, Nigel speaks directly to the audience rather than being a part of the class. What difference does this make?

Development as a group

Drama is more than words on a page: after all, dramas have been written to be acted out, not just read from the playscript. How would you speak these parts of the playscript?

Now think about how your class read the playscript at the start of the lesson. Is there anything that you would do differently now? Work in groups of four and role-play the scene, using the work you have done so far to help you to work out how you would act out each of the characters. Think about:

- How you would move
- What your tone of voice would be
- How you would say your lines.

Use the copy of the extract on **Worksheets 77a** and **77b** to help you to make notes on how you will play your part.

Plenary

As a class think about what you have learnt about how characters are portrayed in drama. Think of at least one thing that you've learnt about a character in *Stand Up, Nigel Barton* from the way they have been presented in the playscript.

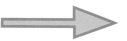

Scene 2 CLASSROOM: DAY

Nigel Barton sitting bolt upright, arms folded, in a small school desk in fairly shabby classroom. (All the children seen later are played by adults, imitating
5 *childish manners and movements in horribly precise style.) Nigel is listening very attentively to the voice of an elderly female teacher. He is, for the moment, alone.*

10 **MISS TILLINGS** You'll get on, Nigel. You'll *prosper*, my boy. You have always been such a *good* boy in class.

NIGEL *(proudly)* Thank you, Miss.

MISS TILLINGS I'm sick of teaching
15 scruffy, snotty-nosed little idiots who'll only end up down the pit like their dads or up to their elbows in the dolly tub[1] like their mums. God alone knows, I've tried in my time to knock
20 some sense into their bony little heads. But I might just as well have been talking to a brick wall.

NIGEL *(reciting)*
I remember, I remember
25 The school where I was born.

MISS TILLINGS Of course you do. You're a *good* little boy.
(To us.) Clever children from common homes like his have to be,
30 shall I say, separated from their – ah – backgrounds. I say nothing controversial.

Scene 4 CLASSROOM

MISS TILLINGS *(repeating)* Clever children from common homes like
35 his have to be, shall I say, separated from their – ah – backgrounds. I say nothing controversial.

NIGEL I remember, I remember The school where I was – torn.

40 *He pauses before bringing out the last word, which he spits out like poison. There is a babble of genuine children's voices as screen dims then dips up for –*

Scene 5 CLASSROOM: DAY

MISS TILLINGS Quiet! Keep quiet, you
45 little guttersnipes! The next lout to open his mouth will write out the Sermon on the Mount[2] fifty times. Understand?

There is silence.

50 **MISS TILLINGS** Understand?

ALL Yes, Miss.

MISS TILLINGS Good! Now, as it is a Friday today, I will not read you a passage from the Holy Bible, as I
55 usually do.

There is a repressed murmur of pleasure.

MISS TILLINGS Quiet! Instead, as a *nice change*, one of you can come out here and read the passage instead.
60 And you may pick the reading from anywhere in the Old Testament.[3]

---

[1] special wooden tub in which clothes were washed by pounding them with a heavy wooden stick
[2] a passage from the Bible
[3] the first part of the Bible

[4] bold manner
[5] reputation, status
[6] rashness, cheerful recklessness
[7] self-importance

The pleasure visibly subsides.

MISS TILLINGS Well, now. Who shall we choose to read from the Good Book?

65 *Apprehension*

PRINGLE *(suddenly)* Me, Miss.

ALL Ooh!

NIGEL *(to us)* George Pringle, the class comic. He can't help himself. The
70 whole class knows that he knows all the dirty bits in the Bible by heart.

Pringle *makes his way to the front, comically, for the <u>bravado</u>⁴ evaporates as he approaches the desk.*

75 **NIGEL** It would be an unthinkable blow to his <u>prestige</u>⁵ if he now selected something harmless –

He looks at his classmates.

NIGEL Hence, the excitement.

80 **MISS TILLINGS** And what have you chosen, George?

PRINGLE Well, Miss. Perhaps this bit. *(He pretends that the choice is accidental.)* It's – um – yes, Miss, it's
85 – um – *(And here, a gush of <u>devil-may-care</u>⁶ overwhelms him and he imitates the mixed <u>pomposity</u>⁷ and <u>reverence</u>⁸ of a preacher.)* <u>Ezekiel</u>,⁹ Chapter Twenty-three.

90 **MISS TILLINGS** Yes? Carry on. And read slowly.

PRINGLE Yes, Miss. Chapter Twenty-three. First verse –

MISS TILLINGS Leave out the verse
95 numbers.

NIGEL *(sniggering to us)* Poor, soft Georgie hoped the verse numbers would somehow give his voice an <u>authentically official</u>¹⁰ ring, thus
100 excusing the choice of passage.

PRINGLE 'The words of the Lord came again unto me, saying, Son of Man, there were two women, the daughters of one Mother.'

105 *Great excitement –* ***Pringle*** *falters.*

PRINGLE 'And they <u>committed whoredoms</u>¹¹ in Egypt; they committed whoredoms in their youth.'

Again there is great excitement in class.
110 *The teacher is paralysed.* ***Pringle's*** *voice fades, then thunders on as he realizes.*

PRINGLE 'There were – their – their – breasts pressed, and there they bruised the – the – the – t-t-teats of
115 their virginity.'

Great howl of laughter, broken almost immediately by change of scene.

Dennis Potter (1935–1994) is one of Britain's most respected television playwrights. He was one of the first playwrights to think about the possibilities and challenges of writing plays for television.

⁸ *religious respect*
⁹ *the book of the Bible that he is reading*
¹⁰ *genuine*
¹¹ *slept with many men*

Consolidation (1)

Aims

In these four pages you will:

- Use what you have learnt about playscripts to analyse and comment on another scene from *Stand Up, Nigel Barton*.
- Develop your understanding of the role different words and phrases play in sentences.

Starter on your own

Grammar helps you to make words do what you want them to do. There's a whole range of technical words to sum up the different role that words or **phrases** play in sentences. You'll have met quite a few of these in primary school such as nouns (naming words) and verbs (doing words). These words are called **word classes**.

Listen and watch carefully while your teacher explains the functions of the key parts of a sentence based on the sentences below (**Worksheet 78**).

- *The cat sat.*
- *The hungry cat sat miserably on the mat.*
- *The hungry cat, because it had not been fed for many hours, sat miserably on the mat.*

Now you've got to construct a similar sentence yourself. If you like, you can use the sentence 'The shark swam ...' as a starting point.

Practise on your whiteboards, or on paper. See if you can add words, phrases and **clauses** to your sentence, just as your teacher did, and explain the function of each word or group of words. Once you think you've done it, write your sentence in your books, clearly labelling the function of each part. If there's time, explain your sentence to your neighbour or, even better, see if you can explain it to someone at home. Be prepared to present your sentence to the class.

Introduction

So far in this section you have looked at some of the main ingredients of good playscripts and how the playwright has used these ingredients to hold the interest of the audience. In this lesson you are going to use what you have learnt to analyse and comment on another extract from *Stand Up, Nigel Barton*.

Read through the extract on pages 98–99 as a class, with individuals playing the part of Nigel, Miss Tillings, the boy, Bert and the girl, and the rest of the class taking the role of Miss Tillings's class.

---

clause the building block of a sentence; each clause must include a verb and normally includes a subject as well

phrase a group of words, which only makes full sense as part of a sentence

word class a way of classifying words with the same function, such as verb, noun, adjective, adverb and pronoun

Use the questions below to help you to analyse this extract and assess and make comments on its purpose, plot, character, dialogue and dramatic technique.

Purpose

● Why did Dennis Potter include scene 18?

Plot

● How does the playwright grab the audience's attention?

● How does the playwright maintain the audience's interest?

● Is the ending effective?

Character

● What do you learn about Nigel's character in scenes 18 and 19?

● How do you feel towards Nigel throughout these scenes? Give evidence to support your opinion.

● What do you learn about the other children in the classroom? Why do you think they behave the way they do?

● What do you learn about Miss Tillings?

Dialogue

● Do you think that the dialogue is effective?

● Does it give an insight into the personalities of the characters?

● Does it add to the drama? If so, how?

Dramatic technique

● What makes these scenes dramatic? Think about what the audience knows and the characters don't.

Be prepared to feed back your ideas to the whole class.

Development on your own

Now you are going to write up your comments in five separate paragraphs based on the questions you answered in the introduction:

● Purpose
● Plot
● Character
● Dialogue
● Dramatic techniques.

Use the writing frame on **Worksheet 79** to help you to structure your comments.

Plenary

What are the key points to remember when analysing plays? Each person should jot down four key points and be prepared to feed back in a class discussion.

homework

Complete your comments on *Stand Up, Nigel Barton* for homework.

❗ *Remember*, read your comments carefully and correct any errors. Have you varied your sentences to make them more interesting? Make any improvements and redraft. Write a brief statement saying how well you think you have completed this task.

Consolidation (2)

George Pringle has now been caned for reading out the dirty bits of the Bible. Miss Tillings has asked Nigel to read the Bible to set an example to George of how a 'good' boy does it. In the playground afterwards, Pringle and the other children pick on Nigel and tease him for being the teacher's pet. In scene 18 Nigel is alone and reveals to the audience what he did next.

Scene 18 CLASSROOM: DAY

NIGEL Now I've done it! I've really gone and done it! I shall cop it good and proper. I don't know what our Mam will say. *(Cradles head)* Oh, my God!

*A moment's silence. Then, as **Nigel** crinkles his eyes tightly shut for prayer, gabbles childishly, move out to show where he is.*

NIGEL Our Father which art in heaven, Hallowed be Thy name …

He opens his eyes and addresses us with wide-eyed concern.

NIGEL After they'd done me over in the school playground I was mad, see. Real mad. So I sneaked back arter school, see. And – and *(face crumples)* I pinched this 'ere potted daffodil out the window-sill. Yanked it out, like. *(Sniff)* Then I – broke it all up. Pulled all them yellow petals off, one by one. One at a time. *(Angrily)* I *felt* like doin' it, see! I felt like it. *(Shouts)* I FELT LIKE IT! *(Pause. Continues apprehensively.)* Old scrag chops'll be sure to find out who did it. I know her! She'll cop me out, you can bet your life on that. *God knows* what she'll do. *(Closes eyes again. Move into big close-up.)*

NIGEL Our Father which art in heaven, Hallowed be Thy name …

Scene 19 CLASSROOM: DAY

Room is full. Teacher out front. Air of tension and fright.

MISS TILLINGS Somebody in this room is a thief!

Silence

MISS TILLINGS Somebody – some wicked, wicked child – has stolen our lovely daffodil.

CLASS Aaah!

MISS TILLINGS Yes, our lovely daffodil. The one we've all watered and tended since the middle of March. Sit absolutely *still* every single one of you. Quite, quite still! I have my own ways of finding nasty little sneak-thieves.

*A long pause. **Miss Tillings** stares hard round the class. The 'children' try to keep their composure, scared of any movement which might be interpreted as guilt. Suddenly, **Nigel** can bear it no longer and his hands go up to his face.*

MISS TILLINGS Stand up, Nigel Barton!

Nigel stands, head bowed in shame.

MISS TILLINGS Well, Nigel! Do you know anything about this? I can't believe it was you!

*At this last sentence, **Nigel** looks up, a faint hope glimmering.*

NIGEL No, Miss.

MISS TILLINGS Then what do you know about it?

NIGEL I think – I think I might have had the daffodil, Miss.

MISS TILLINGS *(sharp) Might* have had it? What do you mean, boy! Come on, speak up.

NIGEL *(twisting his head around)* I – I …

MISS TILLINGS *(menacingly)* Well?

NIGEL The stem was all broke, Miss. Somebody – somebody – *gave* it to me, Miss.

MISS TILLINGS *Who* gave it to you?

NIGEL Um. I don't like to say, Miss …

MISS TILLINGS You better had, Barton! And quick about it!

NIGEL Georgie Pringle, Miss.

CLASS Aaaah!

Georgie jerks up in indignant astonishment.

PRINGLE I never did!

MISS TILLINGS Quiet Pringle! *(She advances on Nigel almost cooing.)* All right, Nigel. Thank you. And where did Pringle give you this broken flower?

NIGEL By the bus stop, Miss. The stem was all broken. I thought I'd try to mend it.

PRINGLE It's a lie! A lie!

MISS TILLINGS You'd better be quiet, Pringle! Does anybody else know anything about this? Did anyone see Pringle with the flower? Anyone see him come back into the school last night?

FIRST BOY I saw him go back into the school, Miss.

PRINGLE No, Miss! No!

MISS TILLINGS Quiet! Did you see him come out again?

FIRST BOY N-no. *(Regretfully)*

The 'children' sense blood and start to get nasty. There is an air of excitement. Eyes are gleaming.

MISS TILLINGS *Somebody* must have seen him come out again. What about you, Bert. Or are you mixed up in it, too?

BERT *(alarmed)* No, Miss. Not me, Miss.

MISS TILLINGS Well? Was he with you? Did you see him come out?

Bert is nervous. He shoots a glance at Georgie.

BERT Y-yes, Miss. He wasn't with *me*, Miss. I did see him come out, I mean.

Class lets out a deep sigh of satisfaction.

MISS TILLINGS *(quickly)* And he had the daffodil in his hand, didn't he? Didn't he!

BERT Yes, Miss.

PRINGLE No, Bert! No!

BERT In his left hand!

GIRL I saw him too, Miss.

MISS TILLINGS Where did you see him?

GIRL *(looking round for applause)* By the bread shop, Miss. And him had the daffodil, Miss. The stem was all broke, like Nigel says.

MISS TILLINGS Come out to the front, Georgie Pringle!

PRINGLE *(tearful)* It ent true, none of it, Miss.

MISS TILLINGS Come out to the front! *(Gently)* All right, Nigel, you can sit down now. Thank you for being so truthful.

NIGEL *(smirk)* Thank you, Miss.

A BBC production of
Stand Up, Nigel Barton

Writing a playscript

Aims

In these two pages you will:

- Work in groups planning and writing the script of a play about bullying.
- Think about your use of tenses and check that they're correct.

Starter as a group

When writing or talking you might want to say what you are doing *now* as well as recalling what you've done *in the past* and thinking about what you're going to do *in the future*. The words that help you to do this are verbs because, depending what **tense** the verb is in, the listener or reader knows which time is being referred to.

Look back at the first extract from *Stand Up, Nigel Barton* (pages 94–95). Some of it is in the present tense, some of it is in the past and some in the future. Has Dennis Potter made a mistake or are there good reasons for the changes in tense in his script?

In your groups work out which parts are in which tense and why. Be prepared to feed back your analysis.

> **tense** the way a verb shows whether it is referring to the past, the present or the future

Introduction as a group

You are now going to write your own play about bullying. In this lesson you will plan and write the script, and in the next lesson (pages 102–103) you will perform it. You should work in groups of five and base your play on the situation described on page 101. (The parents can be schoolchildren later in the scene.) Read it together as a class.

Before you can perform your play, you need to write your script. As a group, make brief notes on the following areas, using the planning frame on **Worksheet 80** to help you.

Purpose

- What message are you trying to convey?

Structure

- How will you make the beginning of your playscript exciting? You need to make sure that it grabs the audience's attention and makes them interested in what is happening.
- What kind of ending do you want?

Characters

- Give your characters names.
- Think about what sort of personalities your characters will have and how you want the audience to feel towards them: will they feel sympathy or anger?
- You need to convey their characters through the dialogue and their actions.

Dialogue

- What will your characters say and how will they say it?

Dramatic techniques

- How will you make the scene dramatic to keep the audience's interest?
- Will you have moments of tension when the audience isn't sure what will happen?

Roles

Director
Parents (to be played by Girl 2 and Boy 2)
Girl 1, Girl 2, Boy 1, Boy 2

Girl 1 listens to parents arguing. They turn on her, and she runs off to school. She arrives at school angry, sees a mate (Girl 2) and spots two younger boys (Boy 1 and Boy 2).

The girls approach the boys. They start taunting and threatening the boys, demanding money. Boy 1 refuses. Boy 2 begins to run. They empty Boy 1's bag on the ground and kick his books everywhere before running off. Boy 1 left alone, making plans for revenge.

Development as a group

Now you need to write your playscript, using the notes you have made. Use your whiteboards or a piece of paper to help you draft ideas. Work together as a group to produce one playscript to be performed in the next lesson. Each of you should have a copy of the script. Your playscript should be set out correctly, so remind yourself how to do this by looking at page 85. Remember:

- **Setting:** details about the setting should be brief, in brackets and separate from the dialogue.
- **Stage directions:** these indicate how a character says their words (e.g. *moodily*, *angrily*) and how they move (e.g. *cradles head*). They also indicate what happens and how it happens, which can help to create tension (e.g. *She advances on Nigel, almost cooing*). They appear in brackets after or before the dialogue, and are brief.
- **Characters:** the names should always appear on the left-hand side of the page.
- **Dialogue:** this should be lifelike, that is, the way people actually speak.

> **!** Give everyone their roles before writing the script. As you get used to your role, the script will flow easily.

Plenary

Each group should think carefully about the things they learnt and the things they found difficult when writing their playscript. Pool your ideas, then elect a spokesperson to feed back to the class.

Performing your play

Aims

In these two pages you will:

- Consider some of the techniques of storytelling.
- Work together effectively to rehearse and perform the play you've scripted.
- Review the performances of other groups.

Starter on your own

Listen as your teacher recounts a story of something that has happened to them. Think about the following as they tell their story under the following headings:

- **Content:** What is it about? Does it contain lots of descriptive detail?
- **Language used:** Is it formal or informal?
- **Pace:** Do they vary how quickly they tell their story?
- **Tone:** What tone of voice do they use? Do they vary it? What effect does this have?
- **Emphasis:** Do they emphasize some words? What effect does this have?

as a group

1 Discuss what you noticed about the content of the story and the way it was told.

2 What do you think the difference is between a written story and a spoken story?

3 How can you bring the words in a playscript alive?

Introduction as a group

Look again at the scripts you worked on in the last lesson (pages 100–101). Each member in the group should take the role of one of the characters, and one person should be the **director** of the production. Practise your scene together. Think about the way the story was told in the starter activity and remember that the way you say your lines and the way you move can make the scene more dramatic. Think about:

- **Tone of voice:** Change your tone of voice to help convey a feeling.
- **Pace:** Speeding up or slowing down what you are saying adds dramatic effect.
- **Pauses:** These can add suspense and drama – keeping the audience guessing about what might come next.
- **Body language:** This can express how a character is feeling without them saying anything.

The director should watch the performance and advise on what could be improved in the way the scene is performed.

When you are all ready, you will be asked to perform your scene to the rest of the class, who will be watching the performance and filling in their evaluation grids.

director the person in charge of the production of a play

Development on your own

As you watch each group's performance, you need to make notes on the following areas, using the evaluation grid on **Worksheet 81**:

Structure
- Does it have a gripping opening?
- Does this convey the message of the play effectively?
- How well does it end?

Characters
- How well do they engage your interest and feelings?
- Are the characters believable?

Dialogue
- Is the language realistic?
- Does it add to the drama?

Performance
- What dramatic techniques have been used, such as moments of tension, pauses etc?
- How well do they perform? Think about expression, movement and tone of voice.

Next lesson you will write a review of the performances and formally evaluate what worked well and what was less successful. Put an asterisk against the performance you think worked best (exclude your group from this as you cannot judge your own performance from an audience perspective). Remember to include comments on how each aspect could have been improved. Use abbreviations to help keep your notes brief.

Plenary

Discuss which performance you think was the most successful, giving reasons for your decision. How well do you think you performed your own play?

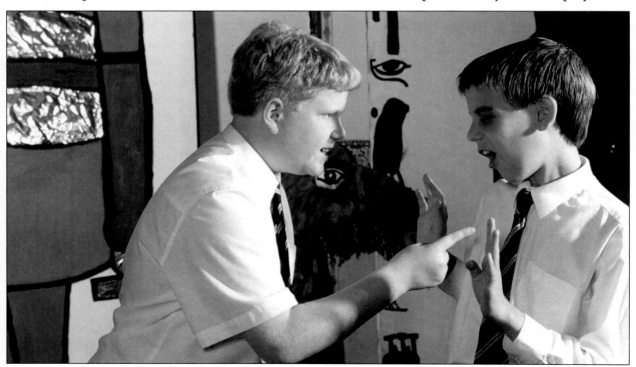

Students performing a scene

Looking at reviews

Aims

In these two pages you will:

- Increase your understanding of how connectives can be used to signpost texts.
- Learn how to structure a review and write your own review, using connectives to signpost your writing effectively.
- Check your work carefully and ensure it contains no careless errors.
- Revise your review after thinking about other people's comments on it.

Starter as a group

When speaking and writing, you use all sorts of phrases to signal to your listeners and readers what direction your ideas are moving in. These signals are called connectives (see page 13). In the section 'Persuade, argue, advise' you focused on how to use connectives to signal ridicule, agreement, neutrality or complexity (see page 62). Today you're going to be writing reviews. These also need a range of connectives, so before you start writing you're going to consider what things are signalled by different types of connective.

You will be given a range of connectives plus seven headings (**Worksheet 82**). Sort the cards so that you have three connectives illustrating each of the seven headings.

Introduction as a group

Last lesson you took notes to evaluate the performances of different groups. Before you write your own reviews, you need to consider what kind of details a review contains. You've probably seen reviews in magazines or newspapers of many types of performance, such as plays, films, pop concerts or television programmes.

Follow carefully while your teacher reads you a review of the film *Chicken Run*, then, in groups, see if you can work out the following:

1. **Structure:** Give a heading to each of the paragraphs, summing up the type of information it is providing. (To help you do this, the paragraphs have been numbered.)

2. **Connectives:** Some of the key connectives in the text have been highlighted – decide what is the purpose of each of these connectives.

3. **Purpose:** Decide what the purpose of this review was.

4. **Style:** Select any phrases from the review that you think help make it interesting and try to decide what makes them effective. Which phrase lets you know the reviewer was bored by the film?

Use the grid on **Worksheet 83** to make notes, and be prepared to feed back your ideas.

Development on your own

Now write your own review of whichever performance about bullying you think worked best. Use the notes you took to help you. You could use a similar structure to the *Chicken Run* example:

- Introductory paragraph – also used to hook the readers' interest

- Background
- Outline of chief features
- General comment
- Personal comment.

> **!** **Remember** to read your work carefully, improve it if necessary, and write a brief comment on how well you think you have completed the task.

Plenary

In pairs read each other's reviews and discuss how they could be improved. Check that any pronouns used do not confuse the reader. In particular, check that your connectives effectively signal direction for the reader.

homework

Write a review of a film that you've really enjoyed – or hated – using the structure that you have worked on. Remember to check your work in the same way. Make any final amendments and comment on how well you think you have completed this task.

---

[1] Hope, Emily Dickinson[1] once said, is the thing with feathers. But hope is in short supply for the fine feathered stars of *Chicken Run*, a new stop-motion animation[2] feature done by British animators Nick Park and Peter Lord in the painstaking style known as stop motion.

[2] **You probably don't know** Park and Lord by name, **but you may know** their work: *Wallace & Gromit*, an award-winning series of shorts[3] based on the adventures of a daft inventor and his resourceful dog, or *Creature Comforts*, a truly marvellous, Oscar-winning short featuring interviews with some claymated zoo residents.

[3] **However,** whether a feature-length animation, neatly described by one reviewer as *'The Great Escape*[4] but with chickens', will fly is uncertain. Set on a threatening chicken farm some time in the 1950s, **the movie begins** with some rather clever connections to the Steve McQueen classic. See, these biddies have to produce a certain number of eggs per week or else they end up as dinner. **No wonder** plucky Ginger (voiced by Julia Sawalha, the star of *Absolutely Fabulous*) wants out – and often ends up, à la[5] McQueen, in solitary confinement. (There's a

great joke in which we hear her tossing a baseball, as McQueen did, to pass the time.) **Things go from bad to worse** when the farm's resident villainess, Mrs Tweedy (Miranda Richardson), decides there's more money in chickens than eggs. She installs a frightening machine that converts chickens into chicken pies. **Enter** an unlikely rescuer: a rooster named Rocky (voiced by Mel Gibson), who claims he can teach the hens to fly to freedom.

[4] **There's no question** that animation enthusiasts will flock (sorry) to *Chicken Run*. Otherwise, it's hard to peg[6] the film's intended audience. **Certainly not** kids, who won't get the movie in-jokes or the deadpan[7] British-housewife humour. **And probably** not mainstream moviegoers, who may find the film visually inventive but narratively slight.[8]

[5] **Still, you never know what** will catch the public's fancy. I was ready to fly the coop long before the 82 minutes were up, but if you're in the mood for something offbeat and wacky, *Chicken Run* may be just your kind of birdbrained entertainment.

Eleanor Ringel Gillespie, Cox News Service

---

[1] American poet
[2] a film that makes successive shots of models to create the illusion of movement
[3] short films
[4] famous Second World War film, starring Steve McQueen
[5] like
[6] pin down, identify
[7] understated, with a straight face
[8] with a weak storyline

Improvising a sketch

Aims

In these two pages you will:

- Look at comedy sketches as a genre of drama.
- Work in a group to improvise a sketch successfully, maintaining the audience's interest.
- Evaluate which group achieved the most successful improvisation.

Starter *as a group*

Your teacher will divide you into two teams and then give everyone a card with just one brief instruction on it (**Worksheet 84**). Read it, then place it face down in front of you. Without using any words you have got to communicate the mood on your card so the rest of your team can identify the mood.

Introduction *as a class*

Today, you will pull together all the dramatic skills you've been working on in this section by **improvising** a short **sketch**. Sketches are usually very short, lasting only about five minutes, which means that there are a number of different sketches in any one comedy show. Sometimes the same character appears in every episode of the comedy show – the audience must be able to identify with such characters.

improvising making something up as you go along
sketch a short piece of humorous drama, usually part of a comedy show

The script on page 107 is taken from a sketch in *The Fast Show*. In it Competitive Dad is playing Monopoly with his wife and son. Read it as a class, with someone reading the parts of the dad, mother and son.

After you have read it, discuss the following questions:

1 Are the beginning and ending of the sketch effective?
2 Why is the character of Competitive Dad funny?
3 The mother and son hardly say anything. Why are they in the sketch?
4 How does the dialogue add to the humour?
5 How would you act out this sketch to emphasize the humour?

Development *as a group*

You are now going to improvise your own sketch using the characters from the Competitive Dad sketch. In threes, take on the role of Competitive Dad, Mother and Son. Improvise one of the following sketches:

Scene: The family is playing football in the park.
Opening line:
COMPETITIVE DAD Let's see how you score a goal.

Scene: The family is watching a quiz show on television.
Opening line:
MOTHER I don't know how they remember all those facts.

Scene: The son is doing his homework.
Opening line:
SON Mum, can you help me with this?

Remember that the purpose of your sketch is to entertain your audience and make them laugh. Think about how you will:

- Open and close the sketch
- Portray the characters
- Use dialogue to add to the humour
- Perform the sketch to make it as funny as possible.

Make sure everyone in your group knows what they are doing and then act out your scene to the rest of the class. The rest of the class should use the evaluation grid on **Worksheet 85** to make notes on the performances.

> **!** You may want to open or close your sketch with a freeze frame – create a still image that sums up the situation.

Plenary

Discuss which improvisation worked best and why.

homework

Use the notes you made on the performance to write a review of the sketch you think worked the best. (Look back on the work you did on pages 104–105 to help you to structure your review.)

The Johnstone family are sitting around the coffee table in their living room, playing a 'friendly' game of Monopoly.[1]

COMPETITIVE DAD … right – come on, Toby, your go. Quick, quick!

The son rolls the dice.

COMPETITIVE DAD Ah! Four.

The boy makes to lift his piece.

COMPETITIVE DAD No, I'll do it. One – two – three – four. Mmmm! Mayfair – my property. My hotel. That'll be two thousand pounds please, young man.

Slight pause.

SON I've only got three hundred pounds left.

COMPETITIVE DAD Well, I'm sorry about that – but you must pay the fee[2] demanded. Two thousand pounds, please.

MOTHER But he's only got three hundred, love.

COMPETITIVE DAD I'd rather you didn't interrupt, dear. He *must* learn the value of money. Now – can you take a note, please? Jot this down: at 7.41, on the 24th of October – don't worry about the year – Toby Johnstone could not pay the sum of two thousand pounds after landing on his father's property.

MOTHER It's only a *game*, love.

COMPETITIVE DAD Now, I shall be taking it out of your pocket money – and of course, I'll be charging interest at the current rate.

Slight pause.

SON That isn't fair!

COMPETITIVE DAD Well, life isn't fair.

SON I only get two pounds a week.

COMPETITIVE DAD Well, you should have thought of that before you went jumping up and down on my property. Now, go to your room and ruminate[3] on how lucky you are that I haven't had recourse to[4] legal action. And brush your teeth, as well.

Son sullenly[5] leaves the room. Competitive Dad turns to Mother and says

COMPETITIVE DAD Actually, I think I will give Maurice a call.

MOTHER *Love!*

COMPETITIVE DAD Shh! Just to clarify[6] my position.

Pause as Competitive Dad dials a number on the cordless phone.

COMPETITIVE DAD Hello, Maurice. Simon Johnstone here – sorry to call you at home. Erm, could you give me a rundown on suing members of my own family?

Slight pause.

COMPETITIVE DAD No, no – my son.

[1] a board game in which players try to buy the 'property' on which their token lands
[2] payment or charge
[3] think hard about
[4] turned to
[5] sulkily
[6] make clear

Aims

In these two pages you will:

- Think about how evaluation is important in a wide range of subject areas, and investigate the vocabulary and sentence structure of evaluation.

- Strengthen your understanding of the role played by different words in sentences and the names given to the different word classes.

- Learn more about using Standard English accurately.

Starter

Below are 15 words plus a short sentence using each word. Decide which word class (for example, noun, adjective, verb, adverb) each of the words belongs to.

1 state	Please state your name.
statement	I have written a statement.
2 respect	Respect your elders.
respect	Show some respect.
respectable	He lived in a respectable neighbourhood.
3 invent	Try to invent a good story.
invention	The invention of the internet has changed communication.
4 sad	The man looked very sad.
sadly	He looked up sadly.
5 bitter	The woman was feeling very bitter.
bitterness	The bitterness in her voice betrayed her feelings.
6 skill	They learnt a new skill.
skilful	They were very skilful.
7 hope	I hope the train will be on time.
hopeless	These trains are hopeless.

In groups, complete the statements on **Worksheet 86** and add an example for each. Be prepared to discuss your findings with the rest of the group.

Introduction (as a group)

So far you've considered evaluation and reviews only in relation to drama. But you've probably noticed that evaluation takes place in every subject. Every area asks you to evaluate how well you've done in the subject.

In addition to thinking about your progress, you will often be expected to analyse and evaluate a whole range of facts, information and opinions in each area. Some of these you will have done already in this school and probably in your primary school.

See if you can work out some of the things you'll be expected to evaluate in different subject areas. In groups, work out in which subject areas you may be asked to do the following activities, and give an example if possible.

Be prepared to feed back your ideas.

1 Evaluate how well you have carried out an investigation.

2 Evaluate whether there is enough evidence to suggest that a hypothesis (theory) is true.

3 Weigh up the different arguments for the causes of something.

4 Weigh up the evidence to decide whether something might happen in the future.

5 Evaluate the quality of a performance.

6 Evaluate whether something will work efficiently.

7 Evaluate whether something successfully creates a particular mood or scene.

Development as a group

When you evaluate someone else's performance you often include ideas about how it could be improved. There are often criteria against which you make this judgement, just as in an Olympic diving competition there are criteria about how much splash the diver can cause when entering the water.

To round off this section, you're going to look at some of the sorts of phrases you might need when evaluating your own and others' work.

Look at the following statements:

- *It would have been more effective if ...*
- *We could have created a more believable character if ...*
- *The opening would have been more striking if ...*

1 Working in your improvisation groups (see pages 106–107), use your whiteboards or a piece of paper to help you complete the following sentences referring to your improvisation:

- *The opening would have been more effective if ...*
- *The dialogue could have been improved by ...*
- *The characters would have been more convincing if ...*
- *The ending could have been strengthened by ...*

Once you are happy with your sentences, write them in your books.

2 Now try to reverse the order of your sentences. For example:

- *The opening would have been more effective if we had started with a freeze frame.*
  becomes
- *Starting with a freeze frame would have made the opening more effective.*

> **!** When we speak, we often shorten 'would have' to 'would've', 'could have' to 'could've' and 'should have' to 'should've'. The trouble is that this sounds like 'would of', 'could of' and 'should of'. This has caused lots of people to write the words down like this. But this is grammatically wrong. Check very carefully every time you use the phrases to make certain you've either written them in full or written 'would've' or 'could've' or 'should've'.

Plenary

Feed back your sentences and discuss as a class which ones are most effective.

Remember to use these sorts of sentences when you are writing an evaluation or talking about evaluation in any subject.

Evaluation takes place in every subject

Reviewing what's been learnt

In this section you have learnt how to develop your skills in analysing, reviewing and commenting on drama by analysing and commenting on:

- How playscripts differ from other genres of writing
- How an awareness of audience is key to the development of any drama
- How dramatic techniques are used to bring a play to life
- The importance of plot pattern and structure
- How character, setting and atmosphere are conveyed in dramas.

You will have shown your grasp of these points by:

- Working in a group to plan, write and perform a script
- Improvising a short sketch
- Analysing, commenting on and reviewing each other's performances.

You have also learnt how to review your own work and how important it is to review and evaluate your work in a wide range of subject areas.

Reflect on what you've learnt from this section and then, in your exercise book, write targets to improve your work. You should consider the following areas:

- Spelling
- Vocabulary
- Sentence structure
- Planning your writing
- Reading
- Speaking and listening.

My targets to improve my work are:

-
-
-
-
-
-

Plan, draft, present

Introduction

Most people find writing a formal essay or making a speech in public a scary thought. But if you think through the process and get the right stages in place at the right time then it can become quite easy. This section will take you through these stages, first for formal essay writing and then for formal speaking and taking part in a debate. The key to both is effective planning and, of course, you can't plan effectively until you're clear about what it is you're trying to do. Once you've worked out a good plan it's time to begin the first draft but it may take several drafts before you're pleased with the outcome. And it's always best to get someone else's view of your work. Once you are fully satisfied with your draft you will feel more confident about presenting it either in a written or spoken form.

Key aim

In this section you will:

- Learn how planning, drafting, revising and polishing your ideas are the essential ingredients for successful formal essay writing and public speaking.

The features of a formal essay

Aims

On these two pages you will:

- Analyse the features of a formal essay and consider the openings of two short stories.
- Answer questions accurately, supporting your points with evidence or reasons.

Starter

Writing a formal essay is something that you will increasingly be asked to do in English as well as in many other subjects, especially history. Learning how to approach this form of writing with confidence, and developing your skills at organizing and expressing your ideas will help you to achieve success in many areas throughout your education.

 in pairs

Imagine you have to write the following formal essay:

> Compare the openings of two short stories. Which do you think would be most likely to encourage you to read on?

In your pairs, discuss how you might structure such an essay and what sort of style you would write it in. Make a list of the key ingredients that you think a formal essay should contain.

Be prepared to feed back your ideas. Your teacher will then give you **Worksheet 87**, which contains a list of the features of a formal essay. Amend this list, if necessary, to include all the relevant points made in your class discussion. You'll be using this list later on, both to help you plan your essay and to help you advise your partner on how to improve the first draft of their essay.

Introduction as a class

Later in this section you will be asked to write a formal essay of your own comparing two short stories. To help you to do this well it will be useful to first examine one that has been written by someone else. Your teacher is going to read to you the opening paragraphs of the two short stories on page 113. You will then be given **Worksheet 88**, containing an example of a formal essay based on these two extracts.

Development in pairs

1. Using the checklist that the class created earlier, discuss how many formal essay features you can find in the example on **Worksheet 88**.
2. Highlight, underline and label all the features that you can find on the sheet.
3. Are there any features from your list that are missing? If so where do you think the person who wrote this essay could have put them in?
4. Be ready to share your analysis with the rest of the class.

Plenary

What do you think are the three most important features of writing a formal essay that you will need to remember when writing such an essay?

1

My father often spoke about the pepper-tree when we were kids, and it was clear it meant a lot to him. It stood for something – like the Rolls-Royce he was always going to buy. It wasn't what he said about the pepper-tree – my father had no great gift for words – but how he said it that counted. When he spoke of the pepper-tree at Tullama where he had been brought up you saw it clearly; a monster of a tree with long shawls of olive-green leaves in a big generous country-town backyard.

'A decent backyard – none of your city pocket-handkerchief lots,'[1] my father said. There were berries on the tree that turned from green to pink with wax-like covers which you could unpick and get the sticky smell of them all over your fingers. In this spanking tree there was always, too, a noisy traffic of sparrows and starlings fluttering and hopping from branch to branch.

From 'The Pepper-Tree' by Dal Stivens

[1] *plots of land*

Dal Stivens is an Australian author who was born in 1911. Although he lived in England from 1949 to 1957, he now lives in Sydney, New South Wales. He has written four novels and numerous short stories.

2

Once in the summer-time, when the water-lilies were in bloom and the wheat was new in ear, his grandfather took him on a long walk up the river, to see his Uncle Crow. He had heard so much of Uncle Crow, so much that was wonderful and to be marvelled at, and for such a long time, that he knew him to be, even before that, the most remarkable fisherman in the world.

'Masterpiece of a man, your Uncle Crow,' his grandfather said. 'He could git a clothes-line any day and tie a brick on it and a mossel[1] of cake and go out and catch a pike as long as your arm.'

When he asked what kind of cake his grandfather seemed irritated and said it was just like a boy to ask questions of that sort.

'Any kind o' cake,' he said, 'Plum cake. Does it matter? Caraway cake. Christmas cake if you like. Anything. I shouldn't wonder if he could catch a pretty fair pike with a cold baked tater.'[2]

From 'Great Uncle Crow' by H. E. Bates

[1] *morsel, small piece*
[2] *potato*

H. E. Bates (1905–1974) was an English writer of short stories and novels, including *The Darling Buds of May*, *The Triple Echo* and *The Snow Goose*.

Gathering the evidence

Aims

On these two pages you will:

- Revise the typical features of an autobiography.
- Compare the way that two writers have tried to make the opening of their **memoirs** engage their readers and see if they're typical autobiography openings.
- Consider how these opening extracts reflect the culture of the narrators.

memoirs an autobiographical record

Starter 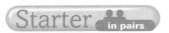in pairs

Today you're going to compare the openings of two autobiographies. First, in your pairs, analyse the three parts that make up the word 'autobiography' and see if you can work out the meaning of each part:

- auto
- bio
- graphy.

Be prepared to share your ideas with the rest of the class.

Now discuss the features that you would expect to find in an autobiography (remember the work you did on pages 34–35). Think about:

- Content
- Structure
- Style, including tense and what person it would be written in.

Be prepared to contribute to the class's list of the typical features of autobiographical writing.

Introduction as a class

Now you will be looking at the opening paragraphs of two autobiographies that tell of people growing up in very different cultures. You are preparing to write a formal essay entitled:

> Compare and contrast the way in which James McBride and Frank McCourt have begun their life stories. Do either of these beginnings make you want to read on?

Listen and follow carefully while your teacher reads the opening of *The Color* of Water – A black man's tribute to his white mother* by James McBride (page 115).

1 In what ways does this extract differ from a typical autobiography? Use the list of features you created in the starter activity and the information in the author box to help you.

2 Now look at the extract in more detail. What has the writer done to help grab the reader's attention and maintain interest? Use the grid on **Worksheet 89** to help you analyse the passage as a class.

* *This is an American text and therefore 'colour' is spelt the American way.*

Development as a group

Now it's your turn to play Sherlock Holmes with text. Follow carefully while your teacher reads you the second passage, from the beginning of *Angela's Ashes* by Frank McCourt (**Worksheet 90**).

Each group will be asked to begin by focusing on a different question in the grid on **Worksheet 91**. Only when you feel you have fully answered the question you have been given, and noted down supporting evidence, should you move on to the next one. You probably won't have time to answer every question.

I'm dead.

You want to talk about my family and here I been dead to them for fifty years. Leave me alone. Don't bother me. They want no parts of me and me I don't want no parts of them. Hurry up and get this interview over with. I want to watch *Dallas*. See, my family, if you had a been a part of them, you wouldn't have time for this foolishness, your roots, so to speak. You'd be better off watching the <u>Three Stooges</u>[1] than to interview them, like to go interview my father, forget it. He'd have a heart attack if he saw you. He's dead now anyway, or if not he's 150 years old.

I was born an Orthodox Jew on April 1, 1921, April Fool's Day, in Poland. I don't remember the name of the town where I was born, but I do remember my Jewish name: Ruchel Dwajra Zylska. My parents got rid of that name when we came to America and changed it to Rachel Deborah Shilsky, and I got rid of *that* name when I was nineteen and never used it again after I left Virginia for good in 1941. Rachel Shilsky is dead as far as I'm concerned. She had to die in order for me, the rest of me, to live.

My family mourned me when I married your father. They said <u>kaddish</u>[2] and sat <u>shiva</u>.[3] That's how Orthodox Jews mourn their dead. They say prayers, turn their mirrors down, sit on boxes for seven days, and cover their heads. It's a real workout, which is maybe why I'm not a Jew now. There were too many rules to follow, too many forbiddens and 'you can'ts' and 'you mustn'ts', but does anybody say they love you? Not in my family we didn't. We didn't talk that way. We said things like, 'There's a box in there for the nails,' or my father would say, 'Be quiet while I sleep.'

[1] *early movie slapstick comedians*
[2] *Jewish prayer*
[3] *period of mourning*

Plenary

Each group should feed back on the question they focused on. Discuss each question and decide what to put in the final two sections of the grid.

Complete your grid and decide which opening you think was the most effective. Note down the key reasons for your choice.

James McBride is a writer, composer and saxophonist from New York. As a boy, he never knew where his mother was from – she would only reply 'God made me.' He finally managed to persuade her to tell him about her background. His memoirs begin with what she finally explained to him. In his introduction to his memoirs McBride comments: 'Here is her life as she told it to me, and betwixt and between the pages of her life you will find mine as well.'

Aims

In these two pages you will:

- Analyse a question using discussion to help you sort out ideas.
- Recognize that planning is essential to successful essay writing.
- Use an understanding of discursive writing to help you to structure your essay.
- Plan your ideas in a flow chart.
- Revise the spelling rules about forming plurals.

Starter *as a group*

Your task is to teach a group of younger pupils, who are unsure about the spelling rules for making words **plural**. Your teacher will give you a number of headings as well as groups of words that match those headings to help you (**Worksheet 92**). Your pupils will have whiteboards or sheets of paper. Decide how you are going to teach your group of pupils so that their spelling of plurals improves. Be prepared to present your ideas to the class.

plural the form of a word that is used to refer to two or more people or things

Introduction *in pairs*

Now that you have studied the two extracts, it is time to start your formal essay.

> Compare and contrast the way in which James McBride and Frank McCourt have begun their life stories. Do either of these beginnings make you want to read on?

The key to success in essay writing is effective planning. All writers need to plan, which involves gathering ideas, thinking them through and selecting what is most relevant. You gathered your ideas last lesson so now it's time to decide how you want to structure your ideas. And you can't structure your ideas until you have worked out what the question requires you to do.

1 Analysing the question

In pairs, discuss how many parts there are to the question and decide what the key words are. See if you can think up alternative words for these key words. Discuss any points that you are not sure about. Be prepared to feed your ideas back to the rest of the class.

2 Working out a structure

As you will be comparing two extracts, your essay will be discursive. As you might remember from primary school, this means that it should be organized so that the paragraphs compare and contrast the key features in each extract. Look back at the grids you completed on **Worksheets 89** and **91**. Use the following key to annotate your grids to bring out significant similarities and significant differences in the key features of each extract.

S = similar

D = different

as a class

Be prepared to take part in discussing the following points about the extracts:

- What are some of the similarities and differences?
- Overall, would you say they were quite similar or quite different?
- How can this help you plan your essay?

Frank McCourt (right front) in the playground of Leamy's School in Limerick, Ireland, circa 1938

Development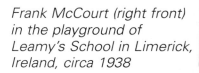
as a class

Look back to the checklist of the ingredients for formal essay writing (**Worksheet 87**) and to the grids you filled in last lesson. Your teacher will show you how to begin to draw up a simple flow chart, and the key point to be made in each paragraph, like the one begun below outlining the structure of your essay.

Structure	Key point/s
Paragraph 1: Introduction	Very different but some points in common
Paragraph 2: Author's purpose	Begin very differently
Paragraph 3: Theme	Both stress how culture affects lives

Plenary

What are the key stages you have to go through before you can start writing a formal essay?

The first draft

In these two pages you will:

- Work together to decide what makes an effective introduction.
- Learn how to write a good introduction.
- Recognize the importance of using formal language in a formal essay.
- Consider the importance of connecting your ideas logically.
- Start to draft your essay.

Starter  as a group

> Compare and contrast the way in which James McBride and Frank McCourt have begun their life stories. Do either of these beginnings make you want to read on?

A good formal essay needs an effective introduction. Listen as your teacher reads you the three different introductions (right), which were written in response to the above question. All these introductions have got at least one thing wrong with them. In your groups decide what are the key weaknesses of each example.

- Look back at what it says about introductions in your list of the features of a formal essay to help you (**Worksheet 87**).
- On your whiteboard or a piece of paper see if you can draw up a 'Dos and Don'ts' guide to writing effective introductions.
- Discuss your ideas with the rest of the class.

Once you've pooled your ideas, your teacher will give you a complete list of 'Dos and Don'ts' on **Worksheet 93**. See if you want to make any amendments to that list.

Introduction 1

> I liked the first one much more than the second one because it sort of interested me. Mind you, I liked the second one when he said, 'Above all – we were wet.' That made me laugh, and the bit about the miserable Irish Catholic childhood.

Introduction 2

> In class we have read the opening paragraphs of 'The Color of Water' by James McBride and 'Angela's Ashes' by Frank McCourt. First I'm going to tell you why I think they started their memoirs the way they have and then I'm going to compare and contrast the themes they've used and then what their characters are like and any similarities or differences in style. I'll end by explaining which one made me want to read on.

Introduction 3

> The autobiography that I've most enjoyed reading is 'Left Foot in the Grave' by Garry Nelson because it's all about football. It tells you all about when he got dropped by Charlton Athletic and then got an offer from bottom of the league Torquay to be a player manager.

Introduction

Watch carefully while your teacher models for you how to write an introduction – getting going is always the hardest part of essay writing. Be prepared to join in with suggestions about how it could be improved. Remember, this introduction should:

- Show that you understand the task
- Be clearly linked to the question given, but not answer it directly
- Introduce the two texts that you will be analysing
- Try to engage the reader
- Be in formal English.

Just before you start writing your first draft, remember that once you've planned your essay, the art of good essay writing is knowing how to begin those paragraphs you've planned and how to link them together. As your essay is discursive, the reader needs to understand exactly what your point is at each stage of the essay.

Connectives are the key to this (see also pages 13 and 62). Look at your flow chart essay plan and, as you write, select the connectives very carefully that will help the reader follow the logic of your argument. You might find some of the connectives below useful.

Signalling difference	Signalling similarity
- is different from	- similarly
- in contrast	- equally
- yet the other	- just as
- unlike	- in the same way
Signalling change of direction	**Introducing evidence**
- however	- for example
- although	- as illustrated by
- apart from	- for instance

Development on your own

Now it's time to begin. If possible use a word processor to write your first draft as this will make redrafting less time consuming. It also allows you to polish your work without being put off by the thought of another rewrite. Don't forget to have your flow chart plan in front of you. Use your whiteboard or a piece of paper to help draft sentences.

Plenary

- What are the key initial stages to writing a formal essay?
- What are the key elements of a good introduction?

homework

Complete the first draft of your essay.

> **!** **Remember** to read your work carefully, improve it if necessary, and write a brief comment on how well you think you have completed the task.

Editing and revising your essay

Aims

In these two pages you will:

- Increase your understanding that spell-checkers have their limitations as well as their uses.
- Check that your sentences are varied to lend pace and emphasis as appropriate and keep the reader interested.
- Edit and revise your essay.

Starter

Many of you will have used a spell-checker when producing a piece of work on a computer. Spell-checkers can be very useful in highlighting words that you haven't spelt correctly and helping you to correct them. However, there are dangers in relying on a spell-checker. Look at the short verse below. It has been checked on a spell-checker that says that all the words are spelt correctly.

> I have a spelling chequer
> Witch came with my pea see.
> It plainly Marx for my revue
> Miss steaks eye cannot sea.
> I strike a quay or right a word
> And weight for it to say
> Whether eye am wrong or write.
> It shows me strait away.
> As soon as a mist ache is maid,
> It nose bee fore two late
> And helps me put the error rite
> Witches really rather grate.
> I've run this poem threw it
> I'm shore yore pleased to no.
> Its letter perfect in it's weigh;
> My chequer tolled me sew.

In your pairs complete the following:

- What's wrong with this short verse?
- Work out which words need correcting (in a few minutes each pair will be asked to correct one line) and see if you know what the replaced words mean.
- Make a list of the shortcomings of a spell-checker.
- What's the most important thing to remember when using a spell-checker?

Introduction as a class

When working on any piece of written work, it's important to develop and vary the structure of your sentences. As you discovered in the 'Imagine, explore, entertain' section, this can add pace, variety and emphasis to what you want to say.

Listen and watch carefully while your teacher models for you how to write a paragraph so that the sentences are varied and key points are emphasized. As you can see from the example (page 121), most of the sentences are incomplete and the textual evidence is missing. You'll be expected to take part in filling in the gaps.

McBride's and McCourt's writing style is very different. The way James McBride's mother uses short, simple abrupt sentences suggests _____. This is well illustrated by _____. In contrast, Frank McCourt has chosen to write more complex, flowing sentences that _____. For example, _____. Another difference in style is the writers' use of formal or informal English. James McBride's mother tends _____. For instance, _____. On the other hand, McCourt has selected more formal English probably because _____. Finally, you would have expected both passages to be in the past tense, since these are memoirs. However, the opening paragraph of 'The Color of Water' is in the present tense because _____.

Development *as a group*

Reread your draft essay carefully, paying particular attention to your sentence structure. Look again at **Worksheet 87** (features of formal essay writing) and consider what changes you need to make to your essay. Use the second column to note down how your essay could be improved. Now redraft your essay bearing all these points in mind.

When you've completed this next rewrite, if you are working on a word-processor, spell check your essay remembering that you should look at each word it highlights before you change it, to make sure it's the right spelling given the context. And, of course, you need to proofread it all to check the words are spelt correctly.

Plenary

List the three aspects of your essay that you are trying to improve the most.

homework

Complete the second draft of your essay and note down why you think it is better.

Polishing your final presentation

Aims

In these two pages you will:

- Analyse the conventions of the main forms of writing you've done across the curriculum this term.
- Comment on your partner's writing to help them redraft their work.
- Refine your writing in the light of feedback given and proofread for spelling, punctuation errors and awkward expression.
- Set personal targets to improve your handwriting and the presentation of your work.

Starter *in pairs*

On your whiteboards or a piece of paper, jot down all the main pieces of writing you've been asked to do this term and the curriculum area for which you did it. Here are some suggestions: playscript – English; review – English; evaluation – science, D&T, art; writing up experiments – science; formal essay – history, RE; writing up investigations – maths, science. Be prepared to add your points to the class list.

Your teacher will give you a copy of **Worksheet 94** (see the grid below). Add each piece of writing to the grid and tick the appropriate columns, adding information where necessary as in the example below. Be prepared to share your ideas with the rest of the class.

Introduction *in pairs*

One of the best ways of understanding something is to try to teach it to someone else. It is also often easier to notice errors and to make suggestions to improve someone else's work than to see how to improve your own. Today, in pairs, you are going to assess each other's work. The checklist on page 123 is used by examiners to mark formal English essays. The **criteria** focus on those things that will help you to achieve success when writing a formal piece of work. **Worksheet 95** contains a copy of the checklist, to help you assess your partner's work.

criteria standards by which a piece of work is judged and graded

1 Swap your drafted essay with your partner. (If your essay is typed, give your partner an example of a typical piece of your handwriting, or vice versa if the opposite is the case.)

2 Use the checklist on **Worksheet 95** to indicate what your partner has done, and make comments about things that you think they could improve. (If you wish to write something on their work, only use a pencil.)

Key writing completed this term (state subject)	Text type (narrative, recount, information, explanation, persuasion, discursive, instruction)	Structure – chronological order	Structure – logical order	Sentence structure Relies on use of conditional (if …)	Sentence structure Relies significantly on connectives	Content and voice Includes personal opinion	Conten Must in evidence
Formal	discursive			✓		✓	

3 Decide on the three things you think they should focus on most and note these at the bottom of the worksheet.

4 Talk through the comments you have both made and agree on your targets, including additional targets to improve your handwriting if appropriate.

Criteria to check

Purpose and organization
- Is it clear that planning has been used to enable the essay to develop in a logical way?
- Have paragraphs been used?
- Do the paragraphs clearly indicate a change in the topic or direction of what is being said?
- Have any formal words that help with structure been used? (Such as whereas, however, finally etc.)
- Does the writing keep to the point of the topic that was set?
- Have some thoughtful or original points been made to interest the reader?
- Will a reader that hasn't read the material referred to be able to understand?

Grammar and punctuation
- Have full stops been used consistently?
- Have commas been used to help the reader by guiding them through the sentence?
- Have inverted commas been used consistently to indicate where quotations have been used?
- Do the verbs and their subjects always agree with one another? (E.g. he was, they were, the writer says, both writers use … etc.)

Style
- Has the essay been written using a formal tone? (No chatty or slang phrases)
- Have some interesting words been used in places? (Words that show an effort has been made to widen vocabulary)
- Has a variety of sentence starters been used?
- Are sentences varied in length to convey ideas appropriately? (Look in particular for an overuse of connectives such as 'and' in any one sentence)

Spelling
- Has care been taken to spell all common words correctly?
- Are the more complex words spelt correctly?
- If a spell-checker has been used, has it thrown up some rather odd corrections that should be investigated?

Handwriting/Presentation of word processing
- Can you read the handwriting with ease?
- Is this piece written in a cursive style? (Joined up writing, not printed with each letter separate)
- Is the writing neat and regular, with no sudden changes in direction?
- Has a suitable font, style and size been chosen? (Not too large, plain not fancy?)
- Are paragraphs clearly and consistently indicated?
- Is bold text used appropriately?

Development (on your own)

Think carefully about the suggestions that have been made and make a final redraft of your essay.

> **!** When writing always:
> Check – revise – correct – refine, before you write your final presentation piece.

Plenary

What are the key things you have learnt about how to write a formal essay?

Complete your polished version of your essay.

> **!** **Remember** to read your work carefully, improve it if necessary, and write a brief comment saying how well you now think you have completed the essay.

Sorting out the ground rules

Aims

In these two pages you will:

- Engage in discussion on a controversial topic.
- Evaluate the effectiveness of your group and other groups when taking part in a speaking and listening activity.
- Acknowledge the views of others and work together effectively by solving problems and agreeing a common way forward.

Starter  as a group

As you now know, planning and drafting are the key to successful writing. Equally, planning, drafting and rehearsing are the basis for good public speaking.

During many of the activities throughout this book, you will have taken part in different types of speaking and listening activities, such as discussion, role-play, speaking to the class etc. The rest of this section will focus on how planning, drafting and rehearsing can help you to make an effective contribution in a formal presentation as part of a group. The ability to co-operate as a group is very important to success here. As a result, in this lesson your key task is to devise a way of helping to ensure everyone in the class co-operates as good listeners as well as speakers.

In this activity, you will be working in groups of up to six people. Each group will be given a number. In addition, every group member will be given a letter from A to F (remember your group's number and your letter). Your teacher will give each group two sets of questions to discuss (**Worksheet 96**), relating to curfews.

- You will have about three minutes for each group of questions, so you will need to be highly focused.
- Remember that it is important to listen to others, as well as to speak yourself.
- Make sure that every member of your group has a chance to contribute.

Some interesting facts about curfews

- A curfew is a law that requires all people that it specifically identifies (for example, those aged under 16) to remain indoors between the hours specified (for example, between 6 pm and 6 am).

- The word 'curfew' is derived from the French word 'couvre-feu', which means 'a covering of the fire', used to describe a regulation that required fires to be put out.

- Britain's first teenagers' curfew was introduced on estates in Hamilton, Scotland.

- An Act passed in 1998 allows local authorities to ban children aged ten and under from being in a specified place during specified hours. But by 2001, no local authority had applied to use the power.

- A government Bill has been proposed in 2001 to extend the curfew to under-16s.

Introduction · on your own

Your teacher will give each of you a questionnaire (**Worksheet 97**) to help you to assess the quality of your group's discussion. Record your answers on your own worksheet without communicating with anyone else, because other members of your group may have different views to yours. Remember to write your group's number on your sheet but do NOT write your name on the sheet. Hand your completed questionnaire to your teacher.

Development · as a group

Now get into your new groups, A–F. Each group will be given the questionnaires relating to one of the earlier groups.

1   Analyse these questionnaires and, using the evidence of the questionnaires only, decide what were the strengths and weaknesses of the group you are focusing on.

2   Agree between you a list of no more than five 'Ground Rules for Speaking and Listening Activities'.

Plenary

Feed back your ideas and listen to the ideas of other groups. Now agree a list of the key ground rules everyone should follow for speaking and listening activities.

Planning your arguments

Aims

In these two pages you will:

- Explore an issue through discussion, considering the pros and cons and raising questions.
- Take on a role and viewpoint that is not your own.
- Work together with a partner to plan and develop a given point of view.
- Test out the strength of your arguments by anticipating what others could say against them.
- Memorize the tricky features of frequently misspelt words.

Starter *on your own*

As you already know, there are many words in English that are tricky to spell because the way they are pronounced doesn't match the way they are spelt. Your teacher will give you a list of 20 tricky words that are often misspelt (**Worksheet 98**). The letters that most frequently cause the problems have been highlighted.

Spend five minutes checking that you know how to spell these words using the look, say, cover, write and check method. Your teacher will then collect in the sheets and test that you can spell all 20.

 If you make any mistakes in the test, add the words you had difficulty with to your spelling log and try and see if you can devise a **mnemonic** like 'Spot a rat in separately' to help you remember these words.

> **mnemonic** a strategy to aid memory, for instance to learn particular spellings

Introduction *as a class*

Now that you have agreed your 'ground rules' (see page 125), it is time to begin the work that will lead to your 'polished' speaking and listening presentation. In order to be successful, speaking only 'off the top of your head' will not be helpful.

In the final presentation you will be asked to express viewpoints and arguments in a formal situation. As you will all be acting in role, many of you will be saying things that you might not actually believe. You need to remember that the criteria for success will not be the views themselves but the way in which the views are presented.

To do this well you will need to plan and draft your ideas in a logical and thoughtful way. Once you have done this, you will be able to rehearse what you are going to say so that you can speak confidently with very few notes, if any, to guide you.

It is always a good idea when planning to present your case in a logical argument, to think of the alternative viewpoint. It helps to clarify why you hold the views that you do, helps you to counter arguments before they have been expressed and prepares you to deal with the views of opponents. When you present your speech to the council, you will want to counter arguments that you have just heard if you can, so the more you have thought round the subject the better prepared you will be.

Your teacher will give you **Worksheet 99**, which contains some views on curfews.

- Discuss each one, and where there are gaps think of the alternative, opposite argument.
- Be ready to feed back your 'alternatives' – whether you actually believe them or not is not important here.

Development as a class

Listen carefully while your teacher reads you the role-play scenario on **Worksheet 100**. You will then be given a list of roles within this **scenario**. Your role will be highlighted.

scenario situation

in pairs

Find the person who has been given the same role as you. Your task is to work together as partners planning, drafting and rehearsing a two-minute speech for the council debate. Each partner should speak for approximately one minute.

Follow this planning method:

1 Begin by brainstorming your ideas so far.
2 Use **Worksheet 99** to help you develop the arguments you will need to fulfil your role. Remember that you should use arguments that would be relevant to the role you've been given.
3 Think of additional arguments yourself.
4 Decide which points are the most important.

5 Decide how you will divide up the arguments between you and your partner so that you each have something to say.
6 Start to draft your short speech. You only have a minute each so it might be best to have one or at most three key points to make each.

For or against?

'I think curfews are a good idea provided parents realize children are their responsibility. It's no good if the children have to stay in, but the parents go out. Prevention is better than cure, though. Young people need to be stimulated. We need properly funded activities for teenagers.'

Headteacher, Norwich

'Curfews are not the answer to youth crime. They could worsen already fraught relations between young people and the police and needlessly penalize the majority of law-abiding children.'

Director of policy at NACRO, the crime reduction charity

Plenary

Why will planning, drafting and rehearsing help you perform your role more successfully?

homework

- Complete the first draft of your speech.
- Continue your research by asking people at home, relations and neighbours what they think about the issue. They may well give you some interesting ideas.

Rehearsing your presentation

Aims

In these two pages you will:

- Work with other groups to refine your side's presentation.
- Decide what are the key ingredients of successful public speaking.
- Consider varying the formality of your expression to suit the situation.
- Redraft and rehearse your speech in the light of comments made by others.

Starter · as a group

- Think about all the times you have listened to people speaking in a formal situation, for example school assemblies and documentaries on television. What are the qualities that you think are important? Think about the way things are said as well as what is said.
- Using **Worksheet 101**, draw up a list of the top five qualities that you think are important for people who are speaking in a formal situation. If you have additional points include them in order of importance under the main list.

The class will then agree on a final list, which includes the best ideas from each group. Remember to note the final list down as you will need to refer to it later on.

Introduction · in pairs

Working with your role-play partner, practise presenting your speech and amend it in the light of their comments. Bear in mind the five key ingredients of effective public speaking and try to ensure that you fulfil these. Remember to consider the right level of formality that is appropriate to the occasion.

Do not read your speech. Work out what you want to say then jot it down as brief notes that will summarize the points you want to make in the right order. Remember that on the day you might want to adjust what you say in the light of points that have been made by speakers from the other side. Try to have the confidence to be flexible and not always cling to the lines you have worked on.

Development · as a group

Stage 1

Each pair should now join up with the pairs on the same side that are most likely to be using similar arguments, as follows:

- The young persons should pair up with the parents. This will make two groups of four (that is, one group of parents and young people who are for curfews and one group against).
- The social workers, teachers and police should join together. This will make two groups of six.
- The senior citizens should pair up with the shopkeepers. This will make two groups of four.

Joining together like this will minimize repetition of the same points and will allow each person to back up someone else's point while moving on to make another. Now do the following:

- Each group should appoint a spokesperson – the spokesperson will be responsible for reporting on the outcome of the discussion to the combined group.

- Listen to each others' presentations and check for overlap or 'holes' in each person's argument – things that should have been said and haven't been, or points that are weak and could be too easily challenged. Also use the opportunity to offer constructive advice on how people could improve their presentations. You want to make your side's case as watertight as possible.

Stage 2

1 All the groups who support the curfew should now join together and the anti-curfew groups should do likewise. Each large group should quickly appoint a chairperson who will then run this meeting.

2 The three spokespeople for each of the groups that have just met should report back on the main points made by their groupings. Everyone should listen carefully and decide if any adjustments need to be made to ensure that the representatives are all making different and coherent points.

NOTE: In the next lesson, the chairperson will also act as the representative of the group at the council meeting and will be asked to sum up the main arguments made by the group. The chairperson should, therefore, keep a note of each person's argument.

Speaking on behalf of parents for the curfew, we want to endorse all the points the young people made. Moreover ...

Plenary

What do you think are the key ingredients for successful speech making when speaking on behalf of a group of people?

homework

Practise making your revised speech as effective as possible within your very tight one-minute time limit. Try to speak without notes or just use single-word prompts.

> **Notice**
> Next lesson your classroom will be set up for the council debate which will be chaired by your teacher in their new role as Leader of the Council. Remember to be in role from the moment you step into the classroom. Everyone will have two roles:
> ■ spokesperson for your group
> ■ local councillor – for when you are listening to the debate.
> The Leader of the Council will provide you with an evaluation sheet on which to evaluate the performance of each group.

The great debate

Aims

In these two pages you will:

- Role play both your allocated role and that of a local councillor.
- Present your case and cross question others on theirs.
- Speak with the level of formality appropriate to the role you are in at the time.
- Answer questions appropriately drawing on relevant arguments.
- Objectively sum up which side has won as a disinterested participant.

Disinterested means not biased, willing to listen to both sides. Judges are supposed to be disinterested.

Uninterested means not interested.

Be careful about these words. You will often hear people saying disinterested when what they mean is uninterested. It is a useful distinction to maintain.

Starter · as a class

The Leader of the Council will welcome you to the debate and sit the two sides on either side of the debating chamber. As a councillor you will be provided with a note-taking grid to record the effectiveness of each group's case (**Worksheet 102**). You will grade each group out of 10.

Introduction · as a class

The rules of debate are as follows:

- The first group in favour of the curfew (the young people) will be called to speak first, followed by the young people opposing the curfew.

- Each group has two minutes in which to put their case. When warned that their time is up, speakers may finish the sentence they are on.

- Councillors will award each group marks on the evaluation sheet provided.

- Councillors will then be able to question any of the speakers but, given the time limit on this debate, each councillor may only ask one question in the debate.

- Any persons seeking to disrupt the meeting will, if they fail to obey the request of the leader, be ejected from the meeting.

- Once all the groups represented have made their case, the leader will call upon a representative of either side to sum up the key points for their side.

- Councillors will then add up the scores on their evaluation sheet and vote accordingly when requested by the leader. The leader may call upon councillors to justify their position.

- The Leader of the Council's ruling on any matter is final.

Development as a group

The debate will now commence. During the debate, remember to decide whether you are in role as a group representative or as a councillor at any one time and act and speak accordingly. Council debating chambers have a public gallery. The Leader of the Council may find that supporters of the various groups have come along to encourage their side and may not always use the formal language that the group representatives will be trying to maintain. Should any members of the public fail to obey the requests of the chair, the council security staff will be ordered to eject them from the debate.

Plenary

The councillors will decide which side has won and what were the key reasons for the success of the winning side.

homework

Councillors are respectfully reminded that the Leader of the Council requires them to submit a brief formal report explaining their voting position. The report should take the following form.

- Introduction briefly explaining the nature of the debate
- Paragraph briefly outlining the strengths and weaknesses of the pro-curfew group
- Paragraph briefly outlining the strengths and weaknesses of the anti-curfew group.
- Conclusion summing up your reasons for supporting the group that you voted for.

As usual, the Leader of the Council expects that all reports will have been revised and proofread carefully before being submitted, in accordance with recent practice.

! ● When you come to make your presentation don't be nervous. Everyone is in the same position.
- You've prepared well so you know that you can do it.
- Only use your prompt sheet – you know what you want to say and don't really need even this.
- Take a few deep breaths beforehand.
- Smile – it helps to relax the face muscles and will make you feel better.
- If you get the shakes, sit up straight and press your back into the back of your chair and breathe deeply – this helps get air into the lungs and diminishes the shakes that nerves can generate.

Reviewing what's been learnt

In this section you should have increased your understanding and confidence in tackling any piece of formal writing or any formal speaking challenge. You should be aware of the stages that you need to go through:

- First you have to be clear about what it is that you are being asked to write or say.
- Next you have to ensure you have sufficient information about the topic.
- Then you have to plan how you are going to structure it.
- Once your plan is complete, you're in a position to write a first draft.
- This will be followed by several revisions or rehearsals, helped perhaps by advice from others.
- Finally you are in a position to present a polished version of your essay or speech.

Reflect on what you've learnt from this section and then, in your exercise book, write targets to improve your work. You should consider the following areas:

- Spelling
- Vocabulary
- Sentence structure
- Planning your writing
- Reading
- Speaking and listening.

My targets to improve my work are:

-
-
-
-
-
-

Preparing for National Curriculum Tests

Introduction

In England and Wales, at the end of primary school (Year 6), all students are expected to take National Curriculum Tests (NCTs) in English, maths and science. You will probably remember taking them in your last term at your junior school. As a result of taking these tests you would have been given an **NC level**. Your teacher would also have made an assessment of the work you have been doing in class. This is called a teacher assessment.

There are eight NC levels (1 is the lowest and 8 is the highest). Students in Year 6 can be at any level, but they are usually somewhere between levels 2 and 5.

The levels are also sometimes broken down into smaller sections called a, b and c:

- **c** means you have just reached the standard needed for that level
- **b** means you are secure in that level
- **a** means that you are nearly at the next level.

These tests and your teacher's assessment of your level help you to prove to others what you can do. They will have given your new teachers in your secondary school information about your achievements in primary school.

At the end of Year 7 you may take some more tests, or exams, to show off your new skills and to see how much progress you have made. This will mean that you can start Year 8 with a better idea of your strengths, and the tests will help you to set a few targets to improve your weaknesses.

This section will help you to reflect on what you have learnt during the year, and help you to prepare for the tests ahead. Remember: National Curriculum Tests are designed to help you demonstrate *what you can do*.

Key aim

In this section you will:

- Understand what National Curriculum Tests and levels are all about, evaluate your own achievement in speaking and listening, reading and writing and examine the types of question on reading and writing that you are given in the NC Tests.

NC level a National Curriculum level – a grade between 1 and 8 which is given to your work

Testing times

Aims

On these two pages you will:

- Learn more about the National Curriculum levels.
- Think about why different types of assessment are important.
- Understand some of the technical terms used in assessment.

Starter

Look at the list of words below, which includes some of the technical terms used in assessment. Some of these words you will know; some you will not. Some of the words have a particular meaning in the context of assessment.

ability	failure
accomplishment	improvement
achievement	judgement
appraisal	observation
assessment	progress
attainment	skills
challenge	statement
check	success
evaluation	target
examination	test

Your teacher will give you the words on cards (**Worksheet 103**).

1 Sort the words into two piles:

- Words you know
- Words you don't know.

Look up the meanings of the words you don't know. Be ready to tell the class the meanings of all the words when the time is up.

2 Sort the words so that words with the same suffix are grouped together. Discuss what you think these suffixes might mean. Be ready to tell the class what you have done.

3 Sort the words into those that:

- Are threatening in some way
- Convey something positive to you
- You have no feelings about whatsoever.

Be ready to tell the class the effect that these words have on you.

4 Talk about why you think these words will be important for the work in this chapter.

Introduction

During the summer term you begin to realize that the school year is coming to an end. Perhaps you start to think of the holidays and then moving up to another year group in September. Before all that happens, however, you may remember that summer time also seems to be a time for testing. No one will admit to liking tests, but you need to try to look at them in a positive way as they help to establish what National Curriculum level you are at. National Curriculum levels are a way of keeping track of the progress you make from one year to another.

What do the NC levels mean?

In order to achieve a certain NC level, you have to be able to show that you can do what the **attainment target** says you should be able to do. These targets obviously become more demanding as you move up the levels. That's why the work you do during the year usually seems to get harder.

in pairs

What must you do to achieve a particular NC level?
In the tinted panel below are some statements taken from the National Curriculum attainment targets in reading. Working with a partner, see if you can decide which level the statements belong to. They cover levels 1 to 5. (Remember that 1 is the lowest and 5 is the highest.)
Check your answers with the rest of the class and see if you can all agree.

on your own

Decide which statements describe what *you* think you can do.

> **attainment target** a list of the knowledge, skills and understanding that you need to achieve in each subject skill at every level. In English there are three attainment targets, one for each of the special skills: **1** speaking and listening, **2** reading and **3** writing.

Attainment targets in reading

i. Pupils' reading of simple texts shows understanding and is generally accurate.

ii. Pupils show understanding of a range of texts, selecting essential points and using <u>inference</u>[1] and <u>deduction</u>[2] where appropriate.

iii. In responding to a range of texts, pupils show understanding of significant ideas, themes, events and characters.

iv. Pupils recognize familiar words in simple texts.

v. Pupils read a range of texts <u>fluently</u>[3] and accurately.

[1,2] *methods of working out what is true on the basis of information that you have already*
[3] *clearly and without hesitation*

Plenary

Compare your findings and decide which are the three best reasons for taking tests.

Development *as a group*

There's no point in doing tests if you don't understand why they have to be done. So in your starter session groups discuss the questions below. Record your own responses on **Worksheet 104**.

1 What are tests for?
Can you think of three good reasons for taking tests?

2 Why do we need tests?
Does taking a test, under examination conditions, prove things that work done in class or at home may not prove? What are those things?

3 What are the pros and cons of tests?
Make a list of the advantages and disadvantages of tests and class/homework.

4 Does it matter?
Whatever the assessment method, why is it important to show what you can do?

Self-evaluation and target settin

Aims

On these two pages you will:

- Be introduced to some of the skills that are needed for each attainment target in English.
- Think about your own English skills.
- Evaluate your success and set targets for the future.

Starter  in pairs

Look at the different statements on the cards your teacher will give you (**Worksheet 105**). They describe National Curriculum attainment targets, at different levels, for the three special skills in English (speaking and listening, reading and writing) (see page 134).

1 Working in pairs, sort these statements into those that you think are to do with: (a) speaking and listening, (b) reading and (c) writing.

2 When you have sorted the statements correctly, try to put each category into the correct order, from what you think someone on level 1 could do, up to level 5.

(Keep the statements when you have finished – you will need them again for an activity later on.)

From working on these statements you will have developed your understanding that English is a very complex subject, and there are a great many skills for you to master. But don't let this worry you! Once you can do something with confidence, it helps you to move on to something more difficult. Sometimes the best way to make progress is to concentrate on improving a few skills at a time.

Introduction in pairs

Working with a partner, talk about the starter session statements and relate them to yourself. Take it in turns to sort them into four categories that describe you. What do you think you:

- Can always do well on your own
- Can usually do
- Can do with a little help
- Find difficult and need to work on?

Development in pairs

How well have you done this year? You and your teacher know that tests are not the only way to show what you can do. The work you have done in English lessons during the year is equally important. Take some time to think about your English work and skills, then use **Worksheet 106** to write your responses to the questions below.

1 What English work are you most proud of?

2 What do you think is the most interesting and enjoyable work in English?

3 What type of English work do you find the most difficult?

Plenary

Now let's look forward to the future. In order to improve, what targets would you set for yourself? Think of your work on the starter session statements to give you some ideas. Then write down three targets – things you would like to improve – at the bottom of **Worksheet 106**. (It would be useful if you could think of one target for each of the three special skills in English – speaking and listening, reading and writing.)

> **! Remember**
> - Be honest.
> - Don't just say 'spelling' – that's too vague.
> - Think about what's important.
> - Be realistic. We can't all become a Dickens overnight – even he took several years.

Speaking and listening

Aims

On these two pages you will:
- Reflect on the speaking and listening activities you have taken part in during the year.
- Consider the many purposes of speaking and listening.
- Demonstrate effective speaking and listening skills.
- Learn keywords that are concerned with speaking and listening.

Starter  as a group

1. Get into four groups of equal size.
2. Each group will be given a different topic for discussion (**Worksheet 107**).
3. After five minutes one person from each group will go to another group.
4. In the new group this person, 'the expert' on their topic, will feed back the results of their discussion in their first group to the others in their new group.

Introduction

When you think about it, more of your life is spent speaking and listening to others than it is reading or writing, so it is important to get it right.

Talking through ideas with others helps you to think more effectively. Listening to others helps you to reflect on and solve your own problems and questions. That is one of the reasons why teachers are so keen for you to discuss ideas. It helps to make things clear in your mind.

Drama will also help you consider how to speak effectively for different purposes, including choosing the right tone of voice and the right words. Many other subject areas will want you to present your ideas out loud. Not all jobs require reading and writing, but effective spoken communication is very important to most jobs.

It is therefore no coincidence that speaking and listening comes first in the English National Curriculum attainment targets. It is the cornerstone of almost everything we do.

as a group

As with everything else, there are special words to do with speaking and listening. Knowing what they mean will help you to focus on how to approach **oral** work and help you to improve your skills.

Working in six groups:

1. Find out the meanings of the words that your group is given (**Worksheet 108**). (It may be handy to have a dictionary at this point.)
2. Discuss how these words relate to speaking and listening.

oral to do with speaking rather than writing

Development as a group

1 Create a presentation, involving every member of the group, that communicates the meanings of the words on the worksheet clearly to the rest of the class. Do this in as imaginative a way as possible, so that it will help your audience to remember the spellings and the meanings.

2 While you are listening to each group think about how you would evaluate or assess their contribution. What criteria would you use? Make notes to be used in your next lesson (pages 140–141).

Plenary

Discuss these questions as a class:

1 What speaking and listening skills have you just used?

2 What speaking and listening activities have you taken part in?

3 How well have you done? (How do you know?)

Aims

On these two pages you will:

- Be introduced to some of the assessment criteria for speaking and listening.
- Demonstrate your understanding by devising a speaking and listening activity and assessment criteria of your own for others to do.
- Take part in a speaking and listening activity created by someone else in the class.

Starter *in pairs*

Working in pairs, look at the series of statements on **Worksheet 109**. They describe speaking and listening achievements from levels 3 to 6, according to the National Curriculum.

1 On your own at first, read through the statements and put a tick against those that you think you can do with confidence.

2 Look at the statements that you have not ticked and choose *three* that you think you should target to help you improve. Put a cross against these.

3 Discuss with your partner what you have done and see if you can help each other to think of ways in which you can achieve your aim.

4 Afterwards, as a whole class, discuss which statements belong to which level.

Introduction *in pairs*

Although speaking and listening are not tested formally in the National Curriculum Tests, these essential skills form an important part of the assessment of your English work during the year.

If you were trying to assess someone for speaking and listening, how would you decide how good they were? What would you look for? Working with your partner, follow the steps below. Use **Worksheet 110** to record your ideas.

1 Think of a short speaking and listening activity for another pair to do that will give them a chance to demonstrate their skills. You could, for example, choose a role-play, or a discussion, or a question and answer session on one of these topics:
- Animal experiments
- School uniform
- Violence on TV.

2 Having decided on your activity, make a list of four things you would look out for when assessing this activity – your criteria. Use the list of statements on **Worksheet 109** to help you.

3 When you have your list, work with another pair and see if you can all agree on the criteria for assessing each other's speaking and listening activity.

> **!** **Remember**, when you are having a discussion it is important to have a good balance between speaking and listening.

Development as a group

Imagine what it would be like if you were a teacher trying to assess a class in a speaking and listening activity. What would be the problems and how would you try to overcome them?

It is time to put your assessment criteria into practice.

Stage 1

Working in your double pair groups, pair A does pair B's task, then pair B does pair A's task. First, in your pairs, discuss the tasks you have been given and think about what you are going to do.

Stage 2

While pair A performs their given task, pair B uses their criteria to assess the skills of the students performing the activity. Remember to be fair and honest – the tables will soon be turned on you.

Stage 3

Feedback time. Using their criteria, the 'assessing' group should tell the 'performers' how they have done.

Stage 4

Repeat stages 2 and 3, reversing the roles – so that 'assessors' become 'performers' and vice versa.

Plenary

Feed back to the class the three most important points that you have learnt about assessing speaking and listening.

Reading: the world of words

Aims

On these two pages you will:

- Develop your understanding that reading is an important skill.
- Demonstrate your ability to understand and analyse what you read.

Starter  as a group

What have you read this year? You will be divided into four groups.

- Each group will be given a different question to answer (**Worksheet 111**).
- Record your responses on large sheets of coloured paper (if this is possible) so that they can be used for display in the classroom later on.
- Make sure that you use your listening skills well and allow everyone to make a contribution.
- You don't have very long – so get thinking quickly!
- Be ready to feed back to the class when the time is up.

Think about the answers that you have gathered together and you will probably be astonished at the wide variety and quantity of things that you read every day, sometimes without even being aware of it. If there is so much to read, and so many occasions when you need to read, you will understand why reading is so important.

Introduction as a class

An important aspect of reading fiction texts is the ability to understand and analyse how an author creates an effect on the reader through the words and imagery that they use. The effect may be one of suspense, sadness or even humour.

Read the extract on page 143. It is taken from one of Charles Dickens's longest novels, *Our Mutual Friend*. Think about the effect this description has on you and how the atmosphere has been created.

Development in pairs

Discuss these questions together. Record your responses on **Worksheet 112**.

- How does the scene Dickens has described make you feel?
- Choose two examples of words and phrases and comment on why you find them interesting.
- Dickens's description of the mysterious effect of the fog is interesting. Using your own words and those from the passage, describe what you think the fog is like.
- Find another example in the passage of where Dickens describes something in an unusual way.

Plenary

Why is reading important? Complete these sentences, and share your ideas in a whole class discussion:

- Reading is important because ...
- Reading helps me to ...

Display your responses in the classroom.

Fog in the City

It was a foggy day in London, and the fog was heavy and dark. <u>Animate</u>[1] London, with smarting eyes and irritated lungs, was blinking, wheezing, and choking; <u>inanimate</u>[2] London was a sooty <u>spectre</u>,[3] divided in purpose between being visible and invisible, and so being wholly neither. Gaslights flared in the shops with a haggard and unblest air, as knowing themselves to be night-creatures that had no business abroad under the sun; while the sun itself, when it was for a few moments dimly indicated through circling eddies of fog, showed as if it had gone out and were collapsing flat and cold … the loftiest buildings made an occasional struggle to get their heads above the foggy sea, and especially the great dome of Saint Paul's seemed to die hard; but this was not <u>perceivable</u>[4] in the streets at their feet, where the whole <u>metropolis</u>[5] was a heap of vapour charged with muffled sound of wheels, and enfolding a gigantic <u>catarrh</u>.[6]

Charles Dickens (1812–1870) is one of the greatest writers in the English literary heritage. He told stories which included wonderful descriptions of the world he saw around him. Using his very imaginative skilful language, he could draw his readers into the world of his stories.

[1] something that is alive, for example a human being, a horse, a bird
[2] something that is not alive, like a building, a lamppost, a piece of paper
[3] a ghost
[4] can be seen or understood
[5] a city
[6] a lot of mucus in the nose and throat

Reading: the tests

Aims

On these two pages you will:

- Be introduced to the assessment criteria for reading in the National Curriculum and the requirements of the NC reading test.
- Compare two non-fiction texts on the same topic.
- Apply your reading skills to write a response.

Starter

Worksheet 113 contains some of the key skills you need for reading.

1 Talk about what you think each one means.
2 Think about how you would be able to show that you could do what is being described and write this in the space given.
3 If you find something too difficult, move on to the next one.
4 If you think this is something that you can do, put a tick in the third column.
5 In the first column write the level that you think this skill belongs to.

Introduction

Reading is one of the finest skills you will ever master. It is a golden gateway to the world. Understanding and developing your reading skills as much as you can is obviously very important. Your ability to read effectively, therefore, plays an important part in the National Curriculum tests for English, as well as in every other subject.

In the National Curriculum Tests for reading you will be given a booklet which will contain a variety of different types of fiction and non-fiction texts. They will include some of the texts that you have read during the year in English and in other subjects, such as historical or biographical texts. They will also have a linking theme, such as childhood memories. You will have 15 minutes before the test starts to read the extracts: you can use this time to get to know them well.

After reading the extracts, you will have an hour and 15 minutes to answer the questions. There could be as many as 20 different questions, which means that you need to be aware of the time that you take to answer each one. Remember to spend more time on the questions that carry the most marks and that ask for longer answers, otherwise you won't get through them all.

It will be up to you to demonstrate your reading skills by analysing the texts you have been given. Each question will have a special focus, such as finding factual information, commenting on the writer's expression, identifying the purpose of the writing or examining the organization and presentation. Some questions will ask you to make comparisons between texts. You may be asked to give one-word answers, complete tables or write longer answers of several sentences.

Development on your own

Read the two non-fiction texts on page 145. They are both about the Great Fire of London in 1666. The second extract is by Samuel Pepys. On page 33 you looked at some entries in Samuel Pepys's diary about the Great Plague of 1665. This was followed the next year by the fire.

in pairs

1 Working on your own at first, one person should study text 1, the other text 2. Using **Worksheet 114**, you should each make as many different comments as you can about your particular text, including:
  - The content
  - Why it was written
  - Its audience
  - The type of text (genre)
  - The expression and vocabulary used
  - When it might have been written.

2 Feed back your comments and observations on your text to your partner. Then compare the two texts. In what ways are they similar to and different from one another?

3 Write a summary of the main points of your discussion.

Fire of London (2–5 September, 1666)

1 The fire that started in a baker's shop in Pudding Lane and destroyed four-fifths of the City. More than 13,000 buildings, including the medieval St Paul's Cathedral, were burnt to the ground. Sir Christopher Wren played a major part in the rebuilding. The Monument, which he designed in 1671, stands close to Pudding Lane to commemorate the fire.

Plenary

Three volunteers should read their summaries to the class (and if they are brave enough, ask for an assessment of how well they have done).

What reading skills have you had to use to complete this task?

2

September 2nd 1666

All over the Thames, with one's face in the wind, you were almost burned with a shower of fire-drops. This is very true; so as houses were burned by these drops and flakes of fire ... we saw the fire grow; and, as it grew darker, appeared more and more, and in corners and upon steeples, and between churches and houses as far as we could see up the hill of the City, in a most horrid malicious[1] bloody flame, not like the fine flame of an ordinary fire. We stayed till, it being darkish, we saw the fire as only one entire arch of fire from this to the other side of the bridge, and in a bow up the hill for an arch of above a mile long: it made me weep to see it. The churches, houses and all on fire and flaming at once; and a horrid noise the flames made, and the crackling of houses at their ruin. So home with a sad heart.

[1] intending to harm, harmful

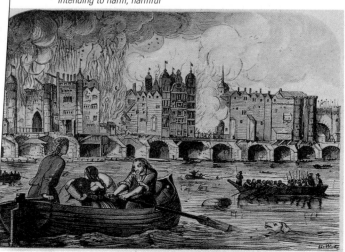

Reading: test questions

Aims

On these two pages you will:

- Examine the types of question on reading that are given in National Curriculum Tests.
- Have an opportunity to answer questions on reading yourself.

Starter  in pairs

How do you feel about tests?

On pieces of paper, or on your whiteboards, write your immediate responses to the questions you will be asked. Don't think too long or you'll miss the boat.

Introduction as a class

The main aim of the reading test is to let you show how well you can understand, appreciate and respond to an 'unseen text', something that you probably haven't read before. The writing you will be asked to do in the writing test is also linked to the reading, so that the tests have a similar focus.

Read the extract on page 147. This is the sort of thing that you might be given in a National Curriculum Test.

In a reading test you will be given a variety of different types of question. Recognizing these different types will help you to learn how to give the answers in the right way.

- Some questions ask you to give straightforward factual information:

  > How long was Floella's journey?
  > *(1 mark)*

- Then there are factual questions where you need to think a little harder because the information is not given directly in the passage. You have to 'infer' or work out the information for yourself from what is writtten in the passage. In the example below, you have to use the evidence in the passage about what was happening at the station:

  > Roughly what time of day was it when Floella and her family arrived at Waterloo Station?
  > *(1 mark)*

- There will be questions that ask you to comment on the structure and organization of a text, including grammatical and presentational features. This can involve commenting on the themes and ideas of a text and how these are developed through the paragraphs and grammatical features. For example, you may be asked to make comparisons between different parts of the same text:

  > Compare Floella's feelings as she travelled into London, at the beginning of the first paragraph, with the way she felt in the final two paragraphs.
  > *(2 marks)*

- Some questions will ask you to show your knowledge of the way language has been used to create an effect. In this case you will be expected to know and use the correct terms for the words, such as verb, adverb, noun, adjective, metaphor and simile.

  > Find two examples of similes that the writer has used and comment on the effect that they create for the reader.
  > *(2 marks)*

A Bewildering Journey

The journey took nearly two hours and as we neared London the scenery changed dramatically. Rows and rows of red brick buildings with black slate roofs and smoking chimneys dominated the skyline. I had never imagined anything quite like this. The houses had such a cold, lifeless look about them, not like the colourful attractive ones I had left behind. But the sight of Waterloo Station, standing palatial and majestic with its numbered platforms stretching into the distance, convinced me that I was truly in England, the land I had loved from afar.

We finally stopped and carefully climbed down from the high carriage. I thought I would fall down the gap between the platform and the train and was relieved to feel solid ground beneath my feet. We gathered up our luggage and as we passed through the ticket barrier and wandered into the cathedral-like booking hall crowds of people started to swarm around us. They came from everywhere, carrying their briefcases and umbrellas, wearing bowler hats, marching like ants, briskly and purposefully. Marmie told us we were in 'the rush hour' and to stay close to her as we made our way down a moving staircase. At first I thought I was experiencing another earthquake but Marmie reassured us that it was safe. Still I hung on tightly as the escalator took us deep underground to another kind of train. I was beginning to feel a little bewildered …

I began to feel drugged on a cocktail of different sounds. New sounds that my head and body would have to get used to. Only my excitement kept me going. I had been in England for six hours but I had experienced more than I thought imaginable …

As we came out of the station the sunlight dazzled my eyes and the noise of the rush-hour traffic made me freeze like a scared rabbit.

From Floella Benjamin, *Coming to England*

(In this case, you will also have to show that you can use quotations as evidence correctly – don't forget the inverted commas.)

● There will be questions that ask you to comment on the writer's purpose and viewpoints, and the effect of the text on the reader.

What is Floella's first impression of London in this passage? You should write about:
● her descriptions of what she sees
● how she feels.

(5 marks)

Development *on your own*

Now answer all the questions, based on the extract above, on **Worksheet 115**.

! To help you decide how much detail to give in an answer, look at the number of marks allocated to the question. You can then tell when a more detailed or thoughtful response is needed.

Plenary

Share three things you need to remember when taking an NC Test in English.

The craft of writing

Aims

On these two pages you will:

- Examine criteria used to assess writing.
- Think about what makes writing interesting to read.
- Learn more about the craft of writing.
- Assess the writing of others and set targets to help them.

Starter  as a group

What do you have to do to achieve level 5 in writing?

Your teacher will give you a number of different statements which are part of the criteria for levels 2–5 in writing (**Worksheet 116**).

- Read through the statements together and talk about what you think they mean.

- Pick out the four statements that you think are the most difficult, and could be used to describe level 5 writing. (Remember there are three levels above level 5, so it wouldn't have to be perfect.)
- Think of three other statements of your own that you think would say something about the handwriting, spelling or punctuation of level 5 writers.
- If you have time, look at the remaining statements and decide which you think belong to level 3 or level 4.
- Be ready to tell the class about your decisions.

'*Reading maketh a full man; <u>conference</u>[1] a ready man; and writing an exact man.*'

[1] *speaking and listening*

Francis Bacon (1561–1626), English lawyer and philosopher

Introduction as a group

Work in groups of four. Each person in the group will be given a number, which they must remember. Each person will also be given a copy of the opening paragraph of a story (**Worksheets 117a, 117b**) that was written by a student in response to the following question:

> Write an opening paragraph that introduces a mystery. There should be one exciting event to hold the attention of the reader and make them want to read on.

Read and discuss the paragraph that your group has been given.

- Highlight three good points that show the student was successful in meeting the requirements of the question – that is, creating mystery, excitement and interest for the reader. (Think about the work you did on pages 18–29. You should consider: setting, narrative devices, choice of words, punctuation and sentence structure.)

- Using the criteria discussed in the starter session as a guide, discuss what you think the student could do to help them improve their writing. Agree on a target for improvement, which you think would help them to improve this piece of writing.

- Write a comment underneath the paragraph asking the student to improve their work by focusing on the target that you have set. (Each student must do this on their own copy.)

> 'If a man write a better book ... than his neighbour, tho' he build his house in the woods, the world will make a beaten path to his door.'
>
> Sarah S. B. Yule, *Borrowings* (1889)

Development as a group

Take your copy of the paragraph you have been studying to your new group (so that all the number 1s are together etc.).

- Tell your new group about the paragraph you were looking at – its good and bad points.
- Put all four pieces in order of merit, from the lowest to the highest. (If you like, you can also give each one a level.)
- Make the improvement that you suggested on the piece of writing you have been studying.

Plenary

Choose something you have written recently. Assess it against the criteria you discussed in the starter session. What target for improvement would you set yourself?

Share these targets in a class discussion.

Writing: the tests (1)

Aims

On these two pages you will:

- Think about the value of writing.
- Examine various different forms or genres of writing.
- Be introduced to the requirements of the NC writing test.
- Complete a minor writing task.

Starter as a group

What is your attitude to writing? What do you think your strengths and weaknesses are when it comes to writing? Brainstorm your ideas in groups of four, using **Worksheet 118** to record your views.

Then discuss the questions at the bottom of the worksheet. Be prepared to feed back to the class when your time is up.

Introduction in pairs

Throughout your English lessons this year you will have been asked to write in a variety of ways, for different reasons and for different audiences.
A National Curriculum test will give you an opportunity to test your English skills and show what you have learnt about these many forms of writing.

Writing is just as important as reading and carries the same number of marks. In the NC writing test, which lasts for an hour and 15 minutes, you have to complete two tasks: a minor and a major writing task. The tasks will be linked to the theme of the reading paper, so you will have at least been doing some thinking around the topics that you might be given. The main purposes of the writing in the Year 7 tests will be to inform, explain and describe and to argue, persuade and advise.

The *major task*, which should take you about 40 minutes, is quite open ended. It will allow you to demonstrate your expertise in writing, at some length, in an imaginative, thoughtful and interesting way. You should then spend about 25 minutes on the *minor task*, which will ask you to write more precisely and purposefully, so follow the instructions carefully. It should allow you to really focus on something and show, for example, that you can summarize your ideas or concentrate on a particular writing skill such as description. Both tasks will expect you to know how to write in the many different genres and text types that you have studied during the year.

One useful way of preparing to write under test conditions is to revise these different forms of writing. Remind yourself what they are and how they should be written. Ensure your success by revising layout and language in particular.

1 Examine the forms of writing and their descriptions on **Worksheet 119**.

2 Match them up correctly.

3 When you have done this, use your knowledge to give more information about the special features of each of these forms of writing, under the following headings:
   - Purpose
   - Audience
   - Structure and layout
   - Language features

● Actual examples that you have read, used or written during the year.

Development · as a class

Working as a class, study the directions for writing below. It is an example of the type of writing you might be asked to complete in the *minor task* section of the test.

MINOR TASK: *Flames in the night*

You should spend about 25 minutes on this question.

FLAMES IN THE NIGHT

Think of a time when you have watched a bonfire burning on a dark winter's evening, perhaps around the time of Guy Fawkes night or Divali.

Write a short description of a bonfire for someone who is ill and cannot go outside, but would like to know about what you have seen.

(20 marks)

You should write only three paragraphs to:

• inform the reader of where and why you were watching the fire;

• describe the bonfire you saw as colourfully as you can;

• explain why you remember the experience and the effect it had on you.

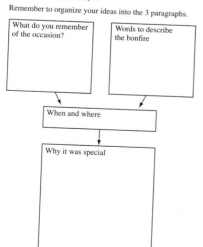

PLANNING

Before you start writing, make some brief notes about what you remember of the bonfire.

Remember to organize your ideas into the 3 paragraphs.

| What do you remember of the occasion? | Words to describe the bonfire |

When and where

Why it was special

---

in pairs

Working in pairs, discuss the following questions before you start to write:

1 What is the purpose of this piece of writing?

2 How would the intended audience influence your writing?

3 Would the language, expression or tone of each paragraph need to be different?

4 What would you need to do, in each paragraph, to demonstrate the range of your writing skills?

5 What would be the dangers and pitfalls that you need to be aware of when writing this piece?

on your own

Working on your own, use the planning sheet to plan your writing (**Worksheet 120**).

> **!** **Remember**, in a test situation look for opportunities and choices that allow you to write to your strengths and show you off at your best.

Plenary

● What have you learnt about the minor writing task?

● What must you do to be successful?

homework

Complete the writing task in 20 minutes. (Remember that you should have spent at least 5 minutes planning, which reduces your actual writing time.)

Writing: the tests (2)

Aims

On these two pages you will:

- Think about how you could improve your writing.
- Examine a National Curriculum major writing task.
- Have an opportunity to complete a major writing task to prepare you for the test itself.

Starter  as a group

Working in groups of four, read the extract on **Worksheet 121**. Then discuss these questions:

- What is the purpose of the writing?
- Who is it written for?
- What type of writing is this?
- What do you like about the passage?
- Re-write any four of the instructions, giving serious advice to someone on 'How to Write Well'.

Introduction

The writing paper is perhaps the most difficult of all the NC Tests you have to take. This is because you have to make decisions on your own about what to write and how it should be written. There is no one to check through your work, no dictionaries to help you, not even a friendly thesaurus to extend your choice of words. It's just you and the paper in front of you. But don't despair, the experience need not be quite as terrifying as it sounds.

Your confidence will improve as soon as you realize that you have practised all the skills that you will need during the year. You have learnt the 'tricks of the trade', so you have all the necessary building materials (tenses, vocabulary, store of adjectives, punctuation rules etc.) to help you create a masterpiece.

 in pairs

Your teacher will give you some statements on slips of paper that describe the aspects of writing that will be used by the examiners to assess your work (**Worksheet 122**). Study and talk about each one. Then each arrange the statements in the following order (from your greatest strength to greatest weakness):

- Those you can do well
- Those you can usually do
- Those you find difficult to do.

When your teacher asks you to feed back to the class, a picture can be formed about the skills you have all accomplished and those that you need to work on.

As a class, discuss which skills you think are the most important and earn you the most marks in the test.

Development in pairs

Working in pairs, examine the major writing task that is set out for you on page 153. The theme of the question (journeys) is related to the theme in the Floella Benjamin extract on page 147. Discuss:

1 What decisions would you need to make before you started to write?

2 What 'persuasive tactics' could you use?

3 What writing skills would you particularly need to remember?

MAJOR TASK: *The Journey*

You should spend about 40 minutes on this question.

THE JOURNEY

Imagine that a friend has invited you to stay with him/her in a different part of the country for part of the summer holidays. The only problem is that you will need an adult to take you there, because you cannot travel alone. There is no one in your immediate family who is able to go with you, and you therefore need to persuade your grandparents to accompany you on the journey. (You can choose to make the journey by car, aeroplane or train.)

Write a letter to your grandparents asking them to take you. Tell them why it is necessary and persuade them that this is a wonderful opportunity for them to make an interesting journey.

(30 marks)

In your letter you should:

- inform them of the opportunity you have been given, telling them why you would like to go;
- persuade them that the journey would be worth their while (even though they will not be staying with you during the holiday itself).

PLANNING

Before you start writing, make some brief notes to help you organize your ideas.

Method of transport and place to be visited		Reasons why you would like to go

→ Why you have chosen your grandparents to take you

→ Why they would enjoy the journey

Before you start to write your letter, think about the arguments you could use to persuade your grandparents and win them over. Remember to set your letter out in the correct way.

on your own

Use the copy of the planning sheet you have been given to record your ideas (**Worksheet 123**).

! *Remember*

- It's a good idea to spend at least five minutes making your choice and planning your ideas before you start. Don't be afraid to throw out your ideas and start again; it is better to do this at the beginning than to get stuck half way through.

- The most important element of your writing is 'composition and effect', which carries almost half the available marks. This means you need to pay particular attention to what you say and how you say it. Your ability to deliberately shape your writing in such a way as to make it interesting to the reader will help you to do well.

- You must plan your time carefully and follow the guidelines that you are given.

- People often worry about spelling and think that they can't write because they make too many spelling errors. Remember that although spelling is important, it is not the only thing that is being assessed. Your ideas, vocabulary and expression, as well as your ability to organize sentences and punctuate, all carry more marks than just spelling.

- Always choose an interesting word, rather than a dull one, even if you aren't sure that you have spelt it correctly.

Plenary

On a whiteboard, or a piece of paper, write down three things that will help you to achieve success in the writing paper.

homework

Spend about 35 minutes completing the suggested writing task.

! *Remember* to read your work carefully, improve it if necessary, and write a brief comment on how well you think you have completed the task.

Reviewing what's been learnt

In this section you will have gained a better understanding of why National Curriculum Tests are necessary, and of the skills you need to acquire in order to be successful. In particular, you have:

- Learnt about the National Curriculum level descriptions and the three attainment targets, so that you now know more about the framework used to assess your progress in English.
- Focused your attention on, and reviewed the skills needed, for each of the attainment targets – speaking and listening, reading and writing.
- Examined the types of question on reading and writing that you are given in the NC Tests, and practised these tasks.

At the end of the day it is important for you to reflect on the progress you have made in English during the year so that you can recognize and be proud of your achievement. Everyone has 'gaps' that will need to be a target for improvement in the future. Now you need to celebrate your success.

Reflect on what you've learnt from this section and then, in your exercise book, write targets to improve your work. You should consider the following areas:

- Speaking and listening
- Reading
- Writing (for example, planning, sentence structure, vocabulary, spelling)

My targets to improve my work are:

Glossary

abbreviation a shortened version of a word or group of words. Common abbreviations include 'Mr' (for 'Mister'), Co. (for 'Company') and USA (for 'United States of America'). You can also use your own abbreviations to save space or time when writing notes or diaries.

abstract based on thoughts and ideas rather than physical objects; compare **concrete**

accent the way in which words are pronounced. Accent is determined by where people live, where they were born, their education and social class. Compare **dialect**.

acknowledgement a formal note of the source of a piece of information or of a quotation in a text. Acknowledgements include, as a minimum, the title and author of the text used.

active the 'voice' used when the subject of a sentence performs the action of the verb: 'The police arrested the man.' Compare **passive**.

adjective a word that describes something: 'the tall cupboard', 'the round balloon'

adverb a word or phrase that tells you more about a verb, an adjective or even a whole sentence: 'Leon spoke quietly', 'The brightly coloured shawl', 'I will give it to you tomorrow'

advertisement a text advertising goods or services, especially in newspapers, magazines, television and radio

advice text that advises; words – either spoken or written – that give information or suggestions for how someone should act or behave

advise to offer information and suggestions for how someone should act or behave in a particular situation

agreement having the same opinion about a subject

alliteration the effect created when adjacent or closely connected words begin with the same letter or sound: 'several silent slithering snakes'

amendment alteration, change, improvement

analyse to look at something in detail as a way of understanding it better

analysis grid a grid which helps you to analyse a text by focusing on the different parts of it [?]

anecdote a short, entertaining story about a person or event

annotate mark up with your own notes, which are usually made in the margin

antonym a word opposite in meaning to another word: 'good' and 'bad' are antonyms. Compare **synonym**.

apostrophe a punctuation mark used to indicate either possession (Tim's book) or omitted letters (can't)

argue to put forward a viewpoint

assonance the effect created by the repetition of vowel sounds: 'green fields'

assessment a formal **evaluation**

assumption a belief that something is true, without thinking about it

attainment target a list of the knowledge, skills and understanding that you need to achieve in each subject skill at every level. In English there are three attainment targets, one for each of the special skills: 1 speaking and listening, 2 reading and 3 writing.

audience the group of people watching or listening to a performance, especially of a play or concert; also, people who read or listen to any texts, whether newspapers, television programmes, books or films

aural to do with listening skills; compare **oral**

autobiography an account of a person's life told by themselves; compare **biography**

balanced argument an argument that presents both points of view in a fair and even-handed way. Balanced arguments are a feature of **discursive texts**.

ballad see **narrative poem**

biased argument an argument that is unfairly presented to emphasize one point of view over another. **Persuasive texts** often include biased arguments.

biography an account of a person's life told by someone else; compare **autobiography**

blank verse verse that doesn't rhyme. It often has a regular pattern of ten syllables with five stresses in each line: 'For he to-day that sheds his blood with me'.

broadsheet a larger format newspaper; compare **tabloid**

brochure a booklet that gives information about a product or service

cartoon a drawing or series of drawings which are funny or make a point

chairperson the person in charge of a debate, who decides when each person may speak

character a person in a novel, short story or play

chronological arranged in the order in which things happened

classification a broad descriptive statement about something. Information texts often begin with a classification: 'Primates are the higher mammals'.

classified advert a small **advertisement**, usually placed in a newspaper by individuals; they are usually arranged in categories (such as 'Situations Vacant') and set out in columns

clause the building block of a sentence; each clause must include a verb and normally includes a subject as well. Some sentences consist of a single clause: 'It was snowing.' Other sentences consist of two or more clauses: 'It was snowing and we were cold.' See also **subordinate clause**.

cliffhanger a situation that keeps the audience guessing what will happen in the next episode of a drama or story

colloquial to do with conversation. Colloquial language is used in familiar, informal contexts.

comment to express a view on something based on an analysis of it

commercial a television or radio **advertisement**

comparison using different forms of adjectives and adverbs to compare things. When you compare two things or people you add the suffix 'er' or the word 'more': 'Mike was <u>faster</u>, but Lisa was <u>more graceful</u>.' When you compare more than two things or people you add the suffix 'est' or the word 'most': 'It's the <u>nicest</u> house, but also the <u>most expensive</u>.'

complexity many sides to an issue

complication a problem which adds interest to the plot of a story

conclusion the summing up of an argument, placed at the end of the discussion or discursive text; in general, the end of a process

concrete based on physical objects rather than abstract ideas; compare **abstract**

concrete poem see **shape poem**

connective a word or phrase that links clauses or sentences and signals in which direction the ideas in the sentences are moving. Connectives can indicate, among other things, addition ('also', 'furthermore'), opposition ('however,' 'on the other hand'), reinforcement ('besides', 'after all'), explanation ('for example', 'in other words'), lists ('first', 'finally'), result ('therefore') and time ('meanwhile', 'later').

consonant any letter other than the **vowels**

content the substance of a text, as opposed to its form or style

context the parts of a text immediately before and after the part focused on, which make its precise meaning clear. Looking at the context (that is, the rest of the sentence or passage) can often help you work out the meaning of a difficult word.

contraction the shortening of a word or words: 'she'll' is a contraction of 'she will'. When a word is contracted we use an **apostrophe** to indicate the omitted letters.

crisis the critical point, or climax, of a story, which the plot has been building up to

criteria standards by which a piece of work is judged and graded

debate a formal discussion in which opposing views are expressed and a vote is taken at the end

description an account or picture of something in words. Descriptions are written in the present tense, and although they must be clear they can use powerful adjectives and verbs to make the description vivid and effective.

device a trick or a technique used by a writer to gain a particular effect; see also **narrative device**

dialect a variety of English, often based on region, which has distinctive grammar and vocabulary. Compare **accent**.

dialogue a conversation between two people, which may be spoken or written. Dialogue can refer to the words that the characters speak in a play.

director the person in charge of a production of a play or film. The director is concerned not only with how the words should be spoken and how the characters move and act, but also with how the costumes, lighting and scenery contribute to the overall purpose and effect of the play.

direct speech a way of writing down speech which uses the actual words spoken, e.g. '"I'm tired," said Dave.' Compare **indirect speech**.

discursive text a text that presents argument and information from differing viewpoints. Discursive texts usually use the present tense and logical connectives and make clear the viewpoint expressed at every stage.

display advert an **advertisement** for a product, often with photographs and graphics, which is placed in a newspaper or magazine by a business

draft to produce an early version of a piece of written work. A text can be developed through a number of drafts before reaching its final version; this drafting process allows improvements and additions to be made and mistakes to be corrected.

drama a performance, or the type of literature intended for performance. Drama is associated not only with the theatre, but also with television, radio and film.

dramatic technique a way of making a playscript dramatic or exciting, such as adding a moment of tension, or creating a change of mood or pace

editorial an article in a newspaper which gives the opinion of the editor

elegy a sad poem or song about someone who has died

emotive designed to create emotion in the audience

entertain to keep someone or an audience interested or amused. Good fiction, for example, uses a variety of narrative devices to entertain its readers.

epitaph the words inscribed on a tombstone

etymological dictionary a dictionary that explains the origins of words

evaluate to weigh up how useful something is in the light of the task being set; also, an examination term which requires you to write about the strengths and weaknesses of a subject

evaluation an assessment of the strengths and weaknesses of something

evaluation grid a grid which helps you to evaluate something, for example a text or performance, by analysing its different parts or features

evidence information stated in support of a particular claim or argument; in general, anything that you see, read or are told that gives you reason to believe something

explanation text a text written to explain how or why something happens or is the case. Explanation texts develop ideas logically, use clear, descriptive writing and connectives expressing cause and effect, and are written in impersonal language in the present tense.

explore to investigate thoroughly. An explorer is someone who travels into undiscovered territory to find out more about it.

expression showing your ideas or feelings through your words, tone, gestures or actions

fact a piece of information which is true; compare **opinion**

factual based on facts and information rather than opinions and assumptions

fiction literature, especially novels and stories, that describes imaginary events and people. Sometimes, however, the setting may be a real place, or the story may be based on a real character or historical event.

first person a way of describing a text in which the writer or speaker refers to himself or herself by using the pronouns 'I' and 'we'; compare **second person**, **third person**

formal language language that pays careful attention to Standard English. Formal language may make use of specialist terms and contain many sentences in the passive; it generally avoids slang, colloquialisms and contractions. Compare **informal language**.

freeze frame a still image that can be used at the beginning or end of a performance to introduce or sum up the situation

genre term used to refer to different **text types**, such as narrative, recount and explanation. Genre also means a kind or style of art or literature, which has its own specific features. Comedy, tragedy and satire are genres of drama; genres of novels include horror, romance and science fiction. Genre can also refer to categories of writing, such as poetry, novels and drama.

grammar the rules of a language, which describe how words can be combined to form phrases, clauses and sentences

haiku a Japanese form of poetry. Haikus usually have three lines with 17 syllables in the pattern 5, 7, 5.

headword a word forming the heading of an entry in a dictionary or encyclopaedia. The headword of the next entry, for example, is 'imagery'.

identify to name something

imagery the use of language to create a vivid image or picture. **Metaphor**, **simile** and **personification** are forms of imagery.

imagine to form a picture in your mind of something. Using your imagination can help you to understand what it would be like to be someone or somewhere else.

imperative a sentence or clause that gives an instruction: 'Sit down', 'Cut the bread'

impersonal writing that uses the third person (he, she or it) is described as impersonal; 'I' is not used

improvise make something up as you go along

index an alphabetical list of items, usually found at the back of a book

indirect speech (also known as reported speech) a way of writing down speech where the words are referred to indirectly: 'Dave said he was tired.' Compare **direct speech**.

informal language language that includes **colloquial** language, **slang** and the use of **contracted** forms of words: 'Don't you eat no poison berries.' Compare **formal language**.

information text a text written to inform. Information texts use the present tense and the third person, make clear how the information is organized and linked, and often incorporate examples.

instruction text a text written to help readers achieve certain goals, especially how to make or do something. Instruction texts generally include a statement of the goal ('How to make a sponge cake') and follow a sequence of steps in chronological order to achieve the goal ('Then cream the sugar and butter'). Imperative verbs are used, and connectives often refer to the order in which the various steps are to be taken ('First…', 'Next…').

introduction the opening section of a text which sets the scene or explains what is to follow

inverted comma a punctuation mark used to show the beginning and end of direct speech or to highlight a particular word ('Look out!' said Dave) (the word 'genuine'). Inverted commas are also known as quotation marks.

jingle a short catchy phrase or rhyme set to music and used to advertise something on radio or television

key sentence the most important sentence in a paragraph

Key Stage 3 the term given to the first three years of secondary school in England, Wales and Northern Ireland

Latin the language of the Romans, which provides the roots for thousands of English words and place names

layout the way a text is presented on the page

lead character the main character in a story or play

lead story the main plot, especially in a soap opera

limerick a five-line comic verse made famous by a writer called Edward Lear. The first, second and fifth lines of a limerick are long, and the third and fourth lines are short; it follows the rhyming scheme a a b b a.

literacy reading and writing skill

literary non-fiction text based on real events in people's lives, such as biographies, autobiographies, diaries and letters

logical following a reasonable, well thought out, step-by-step approach, where the connections between each step are made clear

lyric poem a poem that focuses on an important moment in the poet's life, and is concerned with the emotions evoked by that event

magic e a spelling rule: if you add an 'e' onto a consonant-vowel-consonant (CVC) word, such as 'fat', the short vowel sound is turned into the long vowel sound ('fate'). In other words, adding 'e' to CVC words makes the vowel say its own name. The same is true of CCVC words, such as 'plan'.

memoirs an autobiographical record

metaphor a form of imagery when one thing is said to be another: 'You are my sun and my moon'

mnemonic a strategy or method of remembering something

monologue a long speech by one person during a play or conversation

myth an ancient story of gods or heroes which attempts to explain events or human nature

narrative a text which retells events, often in chronological sequence. Narrative texts may be fictional or non-fiction.

narrative device a trick used by an author to make their writing interesting and entertaining, such as the use of imagery, repetition and descriptive language

narrative poem a poem that tells a story. Earlier narrative poems, called ballads, have short, regular verses with a rhyme scheme

narrative voice the perspective or point of view from which a story or other text is written. The two main narrative voices are first person (using 'I' and 'me') and third person (using 'he/she').

NC level National Curriculum level – a grade between 1 and 8 which is given to your work

NCT National Curriculum Test. All students in England and Wales are expected to take NCTs in English, maths and science in Years 2, 6 and 9.

neutral see **unbiased**

non-fiction any form of text that is made up

noun a word that names an object or quality: 'dog', 'luck', 'Birmingham'

noun phrase a wider term than 'noun'. It often refers to a group of words in a sentence that functions in the same way as a noun: 'all the colours of the rainbow'. It can also refer to a single noun or pronoun.

object the person or thing being acted upon in a sentence: 'Winston scored a goal', 'We visited the Millennium Dome.' Compare **subject**.

OHP overhead projector

OHT a transparency used to display text on an overhead projector

onomatopoeia the effect created by words which copy the sounds associated with their meaning: 'crack', 'hiss', 'murmur', 'quack'

opinion a belief or view about something or someone; compare **fact**

oral to do with speaking rather than writing; compare **aural**

paragraph a section of a piece of writing, used to organize the argument or help readers follow the storyline. A new paragraph should mark a new topic or a change of focus; in dialogue paragraphs mark a change of speaker.

passive the 'voice' used when the subject of a sentence is acted upon by the verb: 'The man was arrested.' Passive sentences tell you what happened and who it happened to but they do not usually tell you who or what performed the action. Compare 'The man was arrested' (passive) with 'The police arrested the man' (**active**).

performance a live entertainment provided for an audience

person a way of classifying pronouns and verb forms according to whether they indicate the speaker (**first person**), the person addressed (**second person**) or someone else (**third person**)

personification a form of **imagery** when an inanimate object is described in language that relates to animals or humans: 'the tree whispered', 'the bicycle shivered'

persuasive text a text which aims to persuade the reader or listener to accept a point of view. Persuasive texts often contain reasons and evidence, use logical connectives and a range of devices to appeal to their audience, such as emphasizing key points and using emotive words.

phrase a group of words, which only makes full sense as part of a sentence. There can be **noun phrases** ('his best book'), adjectival phrases ('not bad') and adverbial phrases ('six hours later').

plan to decide in detail what something is going to be and how to do it

planning frame a grid that helps you plan your writing or presentation

playscript the text of a play, which includes the dialogue, stage directions and notes on the setting; also called the script

plot the storyline of a novel or play

plural the form of a word that is used to refer to two or more people or things. 'Trees' and 'taxes' are singular nouns; 'they were late' includes a plural pronoun and plural verb. Compare **singular**.

prefix a group of letters that can be added to the beginning of a word to change its meaning or function: 'unknown', 'extraordinary', 'international'. Other prefixes are 'in', 'dis', 'super', 're' and 'micro'.

present formally put forward an idea or piece of dramatic, spoken or written work to somebody

producer the person responsible for the production of a television or radio programme

pronoun a word used to replace a noun, a noun phrase or a clause, in order to avoid repetition. 'I', 'you', 'we', 'its', 'herself', 'this', 'that', 'who', 'which' and 'what' are some of the many pronouns.

proofread to check the final draft of a text carefully for mistakes

punctuation a way of marking text with symbols (punctuation marks) to help readers' understanding. The most common punctuation marks are: apostrophe, bracket, colon, comma, dash, exclamation mark, full stop, hyphen, inverted comma (speech mark), question mark and semi-colon.

purpose the reason for something, for example the reason why a text is written

qualify to alter the meaning of a word, phrase or sentence by adding a word, often an adverb: in the sentence 'The water's fairly hot', the adverb 'fairly' qualifies the word 'hot'

quotation a phrase or passage that is repeated in another text to give evidence of something or to support a particular view. Short quotations are usually put inside inverted commas in the main body of the text; longer quotations are usually set off from the text, with a space above and below, and don't use inverted commas.

quotation mark see **inverted comma**

rap poem a form of oral poetry, associated with Caribbean and Afro-Caribbean cultures, which has a strong rhythm and rapid pace

recount a text written to be retold for information or entertainment. Recount texts may be fiction, in which the language is descriptive and there may be dialogue; or non-fiction, which generally retell events in chronological order, in the past tense, and use connectives that signal time.

reference text an information text organized in a clearly defined way (such as alphabetically) and used to research facts and data. Encyclopaedias and dictionaries are examples of reference texts.

repetition repeating a word, phrase or sentence for a particular effect. Repetition is a common feature of persuasive texts; it can also have an emotive effect in poetry: 'Break, break, break,/ On thy cold grey stones, O Sea!'

report a text written to describe or classify, such as a guide book or a report on a school trip. Report texts often begin with a general classification, then describe particular characteristics and end with a summary. See **information text**

reported speech see **indirect speech**

reporting clause the clause that shows who speaks the words in **direct speech**, and sometimes how they speak them

resolution the end of a story, when the crisis is over and the problems and loose ends have all been sorted out

review to write an account expressing your opinion of a book, play or film; also the account itself. Review also means to look again at something, such as a piece of work, and think about how effective it is and whether it could be improved.

rhetoric the art of effective or persuasive speaking or writing; also, language designed to persuade or impress

rhetorical question a question that doesn't require an answer: 'Am I going to take this lying down?' Rhetorical questions are often asked for dramatic or persuasive effect.

rhyme a pattern that occurs when words or the endings of words share the same sound, especially in verse. Rhymes usually occur at the end of lines, but internal rhyme can also take place: 'Who made bats and cats and rats?'

rhythm a regular pattern of sound created by the choice and arrangement of words, especially in verse. The pattern is made by the alternation of light and heavy beats (or **stresses**). **Blank verse**, for example, has a regular pattern of ten syllables with five stresses in each line: 'For he to-day that sheds his blood with me'.

ridicule making fun of an opinion so as to make it appear wrong or stupid. Ridicule is a device used in some persuasive texts.

role play an exercise in which people act the part of another character

root see **stem**

scan to look over a text very quickly in order to find information by locating a key word; compare **skim**

scenario situation

script see **playscript**

second person a way of describing a text in which the writer or speaker refers to the reader or audience by using the pronoun 'you'; compare **first person**, **third person**

sentence a group of words that makes sense. Sentences usually have a subject and a verb, begin with a capital letter and end with a full stop (or exclamation mark or question mark).

sequence to put into a logical order

setting the place and time in which a story or drama is set

shape poem a poem in which the layout of the words reflects the subject, or an aspect of the subject. Also called concrete poem.

simile a form of **imagery** when one thing is compared to another: 'His face was like a wrinkled prune', 'She was as happy as a lark'

singular referring to one thing or person. 'Tree' and 'tax' are singular nouns; 'was' and 'runs' are singular verbs. Compare **plural**.

sketch a short piece of humorous drama, usually part of a comedy show

skim to read a passage quickly in order to get an overview of its subject matter and main ideas; compare **scan**

slang words and phrases that are used in informal contexts, and often by particular groups of people, such as schoolchildren

soap opera a serial drama which is broadcast in frequent episodes on television or radio. Soap operas focus on the lives of people living or working in a particular place, and have many different subplots.

sonnet a poem with 14 lines, often in two stanzas of eight lines then six lines. Sonnets follow a variety of rhyme schemes.

source a text used by an author to help them in their own writing. A note of the source of a writer's information is called an **acknowledgement**.

spell-checker a computer program which checks the spelling of words in a file

spelling log a book in which the student records words that he or she finds difficult to spell, and that offers strategies to improve spelling

spokesperson someone who speaks on behalf of a group, for example by stating the group's findings in an activity

stage direction direction given to actors in the **playscript** as to how to say their lines and how to move on stage

Standard English the type of spoken and written English that should be used when formal language is appropriate. Standard English is the language spoken and written by the majority of educated speakers of English and taught in schools.

stanza a verse; a group of lines with a particular pattern, which is repeated throughout the poem

stem the root or main part of a word, which remains unchanged whatever its tense or number etc.: the stem of 'recount', 'counted' and 'counting' is 'count'

stress the emphasis put on particular words, or on certain syllables or parts of words. For example, 'reflected' is stressed on the second syllable, 'flec'.

structure the way a text is arranged and organized

style the language features of a text; the way in which a text is written, spoken or performed

subject the person or thing performing the action of the sentence: 'Rachel scored a hat-trick', 'The Millennium Dome was a flop.' Compare **object**.

subordinate clause a **clause** that adds information to, or **qualifies**, the main clause of a sentence: 'If you get home late, you'll miss the programme'; 'I spoke to Dad, who was very helpful.' Subordinate clauses cannot exist on their own, but are dependent on the main clause or another subordinate clause.

subplot a storyline that runs alongside the main plot of a play or story, which contrasts with or throws light on the main action

suffix a group of letters that can be added to the end of a word to change its meaning or function: 'breakable', 'posted', 'finest'. Other suffixes are 'ly', 's', 'er', 'ward' and 'ful'.

suspense a state of excited expectation produced in an audience; a dramatic or narrative technique used by writers

syllable a beat in a word, usually consisting of a vowel sound with one or more consonants before or after. There are two syllables in 'river' and one syllable in 'bridge'.

synonym a word with roughly the same meaning as another word. Lists of synonyms are collected in a **thesaurus**. Compare **antonym**.

tabloid a smaller format newspaper; compare **broadsheet**

target what you are aiming to achieve; see also **attainment target**

tense the way a verb shows whether it is referring to the past ('looked', 'have looked', 'had looked'), the present ('look') or the future ('will look')

text the name given to a block of language which has been written or spoken in order to communicate something

text type a type of writing; a way of categorizing texts that share similar features. Information texts and explanation texts, for example, and two different text types.

thesaurus a book containing lists of **synonyms**, words which are similar in meaning. Thesauruses can help you to vary words that are used frequently (such as 'said'), and to select the word with the precise shade of meaning that you require.

third person a way of describing a text in which the writer or speaker refers to somebody or something else ('s/he', 'it', 'they', 'Harry'); compare **first person**, **second person**

title sequence the opening shots of a television programme which gives the programme's title and sets the mood

type see **text type**

unbiased not favouring one side or argument over another, balanced, impartial, even-handed

unseen text an examination term that refers to a text that you haven't read before, to which you must respond and demonstrate understanding

verb a word that describes an action, a happening, a process or a state; a 'doing' or 'being' word: 'go', 'want', 'is', 'feel'. Verbs change their form according to the **tense** and the **person** attached to them.

voice see **active** and **passive**

vowel any of the letters 'a', 'e', 'i', 'o' or 'u'; compare **consonant**

weasel words words that are deliberately misleading, in order to persuade someone to do or feel something

whiteboard a wipeable board which may be used by teachers to demonstrate teaching points and by students to record responses

word class a way of classifying words with the same function. The main word classes are verb, noun, adjective, adverb, pronoun, determiner, preposition and conjunction. Word classes are also called 'parts of speech'.

writing frame a grid that supports your writing by providing the opening phrases of paragraphs